Praise for *Living o*

"Deep. Honest. Transparent. Kathy's stories of her faith journey offer hope to the discouraged, healing to the wounded, and strength to the weary as she turns the reader's heart and mind toward God's amazing grace. The For Deeper Thought questions at the end of each story reflect Kathy's close personal walk with the Lord and provide an opportunity to unleash the transformative power of God's Word in our own lives."

—Linda Carlson, "Colorado 1" Area Director
Community Bible Study

"From the inception of our dear friendship, I've been humbled by Kathy's passionate pursuit of Jesus. In this book she bares her heart and soul with brave vulnerability, sharing personal struggles of heartache, shame, fear, and pain. While reading her stories I found myself holding my breath, uncertain how God could ever bring redemption; and yet there He was each time, pouring grace into brokenness. Brilliantly, Kathy ends each chapter with insightful questions to challenge us and help us reflect on our own journey of *Living on the Thinnest Edge.*"

—RoseAnne Sather, Art Director
Children's Ministry Magazine/Group Publishing

"Through each real-life story, Kathy Loudenburg shares her most intimate problems that have afflicted all of us—suffering and sin. With an open heart, she shares how The One who knows temptations and hardships wants to enter into our suffering and forgive our sins. With humility and love, she leads us even deeper in thought with questions designed to encourage and mobilize us."

—Lauretta Moll, MARC, CPE IV, CAC III
Pastoral Chaplain and Addiction Counselor
at Valley Hope Association in Colorado
providing alcohol, drug, and related treatment services

"We seldom realize just how thin the edge is upon which we live. It is too easy to let our journeys be defined by a fallen world and the limits of our own efforts. With vulnerability, honesty, and creativity, *Living on the Thinnest Edge* gives testimony to the mystery of God's working in a heart that is open to Him. The depth of these testimonies reveals the miracle and wonder of God's presence on the thinnest of edges. I have been inspired to a deeper trust and expectation that God will work in creative, unexpected, and faith-strengthening ways."

—Michael E. Littlefield, OMF (U.S.) President
and National Director

Living
ON THE
Thinnest
EDGE
finding strength to carry on

Kathy Loudenburg

3rd CHAPTER PRESS

Living
ON THE
Thinnest
EDGE

ISBN-13: 978-0-9977353-0-7

ISBN-10: 0-9977353-0-9

Library of Congress Control Number: 2016954928

Unless otherwise noted, all Scripture quotations are taken from the *New American Standard Bible*, © Copyright 1960, 1962, 1963, 1968, 1971, 1972, 1975, 1977, 1995 by The Lockman Foundation. Used by permission.

Scripture verses marked KJV are taken from the *King James Version* of the Bible.

Scripture verses marked NIV are taken from the *Holy Bible, New International Version*®. *NIV*®. Copyright © 1973, 1978, 1984, by International Bible Society. Used by permission of Zondervan. All rights reserved.

Scripture verses marked MSG are from *THE MESSAGE*. Copyright © by Eugene H. Peterson 1993, 1994, 1995, 1996, 2000, 2001, 2002. Used by permission of NavPress Publishing Group.

Printed in the United States of America

Cover Photo and Song Lyrics © – Kathy Loudenburg, Nederland, CO

Cover Designer – RoseAnne Sather, Greeley, CO

Typesetter – Michelle Kenny, Westlake Village, CA

Sketch Artist – Michael Littlefield, Highlands Ranch, CO

3rd CHAPTER PRESS
6542 Owens Ct.
Arvada, CO 80004

Dedicated To . . .

The One
Who makes the crooked straight
Isaiah 45:2

Table of Contents

Acknowledgments

How can I begin to thank all those who've stood with me through so many ups and downs, and people who have loved me so well? Thanks to my cousin, Pat, for saving my life and leading me to the Lord; and thanks to my sister, Margie, and Danny for suggesting the title for this book. I am thankful for Gwynne Mohl who edited these stories, kept me on track, and found the right words when I couldn't; and for Fran MacAnally, who encouraged me all along the way. Thank you, Rhonda Littlefield and RoseAnne Sather, precious YWAM friends, for living many of these accounts with me and for your decades of love. A special thanks to Michael Littlefield for sharing his artistic gift in the sketches, and to Betsy and Jack, who sent me to a writing conference where I literally bumped into Andrea Sims, a friend from forty years ago, who saw value in these true stories and believed they should be published. Most of all, I am thankful for the Lord Jesus who interrupted my suicide attempt, began the healing process, and who continues giving me an abundant life filled with great surprises and amazing restoration.

Introduction

Tragedy gives no notice. It strikes in an instant turning our lives upside down. Thrilled about being pregnant—then the miscarriage. Excited about retirement—then the doctor calls with a deadly diagnosis. Celebrating thirty years of marriage—then the adultery is exposed. Getting that great promotion—then downsizing cuts your job. A phone call saying a loved one has been in a horrible accident or has committed suicide. Finding out about the childhood abuse. News of another mass shooting or terrorist attack.

Life is fragile. *Living on the Thinnest Edge* recounts true stories of hope in despair, victory after defeat, and peace in pain. It is a book about overcoming, being restored, and finding strength to carry on.

Read on to discover encouragement and practical ways to move through brokenness into wholeness.

Part One

$\mathcal{K}$ept!

My folks moved to Windsor, but I stayed in Denver to finish my second year at Metro State. I was determined that my second year would be better, so I cut my work schedule back and lightened my class load just a bit. I made a few safe friends and inched my way through the first semester. I settled into a smooth routine and a great major: Physical Education with a coaching/sports injuries emphasis. I loved the kinesiology classes, the competition, the training, and the instructors.

Things had been rocky in my high school years, and the intense struggle continued into my first year of college. All of that was still very fresh in my mind. I had thought that I could handle a full course load and a full-time job, but a deep emotional wound had worn me to the ground. I felt like things were beginning to turn around; I had hope until I took a very sharp wrong turn. It started like this.

Mom called to ask a favor. When she left her job in Denver to go to work for Eastman Kodak, she left a good friend behind, a young woman who saw Mom as her mentor and a counselor of sorts. Mom stayed in contact with Dena through regular phone calls, but she was worried about her and wanted me to befriend her.

"I'm not so sure I want to do that, Mom. I'm busy with school and work and have very little free time on my hands." That's the best I could do. What I really wanted to say was that it would be dangerous for me, but I knew Mom wouldn't get that. She didn't know about my homosexual tendencies or about a short but heartbreaking lesbian relationship in high school that had ruptured my heart. She didn't know that my nose was just above water.

"Well, Dena desperately needs a friend, and you two have a lot in common. Would you at least call her?"

Dena, desperate? That's the last thing I need! But I couldn't say it. I'd never been able to say no to my mom, so I caved in and scribbled down Dena's number. Days came and went, but Mom didn't forget. After the fourth "hint," I gave in and called Dena. We set a day to meet for lunch.

We ate and chatted about this and that but mostly about Mom and how much Dena missed her, the sorrow in her eyes inescapable. A quiet resolve to replace that sorrow took me captive, and our friendship was off and running.

Mom was right. We did have things in common. We hiked, fished, and camped on the weekends when I could squeeze it in. Our weekly phone conversations became daily. Gradually, her sorrow lifted, and my weekly updates with Mom included much good news. I was happy for Dena and thrilled for Mom. The weight she had carried for Dena vanished. It was my weight now, and I didn't mind.

But something began gnawing at me. I tried to ignore it, said nothing to Mom or Dena, and we kind of limped through the next several months. Deep down, I knew I needed wisdom, and eventually it became clear that I needed God's wisdom. I mean, I had gone to Catholic school until eighth grade and did know a smattering about God; but at nineteen, I sure didn't know anything about discernment. My four years in the Denver Public School System had shocked me into a little reality, but I was still somewhat naïve and certainly knew nothing about spiritual warfare. Actually, I didn't even know such a thing existed.

Anyway, by degrees, things turned dimmer, then dark. I knew what she wanted because I had been there before and I did not want to go there.

Dena asked me to come to her house for lunch one Saturday. I knew she lived in the heart of Denver in an old apartment building near downtown. Metro State had no campus when I attended, so I knew Denver well; my classes were all over the city. I think I paid more in parking tickets than tuition my first year.

So, I arrived, somewhat hesitantly, and pressed the button to gain entrance. A voice answered that gave me the willies. "Come . . . in." I should have run right then.

"D-d-dena?" I stuttered.

"Come . . . in . . . , Kathy."

I entered the run-down building, took the stairs to the third floor, and found Dena waiting for me at the end of a dimly lit hall. I squinted and paused, coaxing my eyes to adjust to the darkness. The inner trembling continued. When she closed the door behind me, the thud made my stomach flip. Somehow I knew that things were not right and that I was in over my head.

"Hey. How are ya?" I ventured rather timidly.

"Great. Just grrreat." Dena's response was like a weird declaration—unlike our usual conversation.

Two large candles and a few small ones lit the room, sending contorted shadows across the dark walls. I couldn't tell if they were the darkest purple I'd ever seen or just plain black.

Swallowing hard, I sat in an overstuffed chair that seemed to suck me down deep. A crooked smile bent Dena's lips, and she retreated into the kitchen to bring out lunch.

Thoughts whirled in my head like ice in a high-speed blender. I was in trouble with no idea what to do. So I started saying the rosary—or a "revised" version of it—"Our Father, help!" I was pretty sure He wasn't offended, so I just repeated it as fast as my fear let me.

In the darkness of that room, crazy pictures on the walls began to take shape and glow as they drank in the candle light. Thick dark fabric took the place of doors into unlit rooms. Shelves lined with books covered the walls. As my focus intensified, I strained to read a title that began with the word witchcraft, but Dena reentered, setting what appeared to be a fat mug of soup on the table next to me.

She sat and slid her spoon into her mug, watching me out of the corner of her eye. A crazy thought about poisoned soup shot through my mind, but I sunk my spoon into my mug, too. The knots in my stomach left room for only half of my soup, and then I mumbled something about needing to study. That crooked and unfamiliar smile returned, and Dena rose to show me out.

I raced down the stairs and flew out the main door into the sunlight. Breathless. I had met something evil. I knew that. "Now what?" I whispered and turned to look up at the third-floor window. Dena, through parted black curtains, was watching me; then she slipped out of sight.

I threw myself into school and work and ignored Mom's phone calls. No update on *this* encounter. Way too weird to share with anyone. I hoped time would erase its memory altogether.

Over the next month, Dena's calls each week were light-hearted, friendly, and fun, like the young woman I thought I'd met. Each conversation softened the edges of that dark lunch in her apartment, and we began spending a little time together again. I methodically dismantled and discounted the lunch encounter and had almost forgotten it as winter approached.

Then it blasted back into full view.

I wanted to go fishing one more time, so two of my friends and Dena and I headed to the mountains. My favorite stream on the western slope had been calling me for weeks. We made camp quickly and hit the water. Up and down the river we could hear the whooping and hollering each time one of us had a bite. There's no better way to end a great day than by frying fresh trout on a campfire and exaggerating each and every catch, the stories getting wilder with each additional log.

Dena's silence made me uneasy, but I tried to pass it off. I mean, she didn't know any of my friends, so it was no wonder she was silent, right?

We only had two days, so the moment the sun smiled on us the following morning, we raced through the willows to catch the early morning shadows of the river bends, exactly where native brown trout like to hide. I didn't notice who went where. I was focused entirely on fishing.

The plan was that whoever craved lunch first would whistle so we'd head back together. As if on cue, as the sun passed over us, a whistle split the silence. Wrestling through the willows with our catch, we each burst into the open, giggling, bragging about our trout, and chattering like chipmunks.

Dena greeted us with her hand beside her face, blood squirting out of a finger that had been cut off. My small axe stuck in a stump, bloody, most of her forefinger lying next to it. Not one stick of cut wood around. That crooked smile playing on her lips. The black was back.

The willies smashed through my gut. I almost fainted. My friends ran to help her, having no idea that she had cut it off on purpose. She showed no signs of pain. She just smiled— if you could call it that—and her steel-blue eyes bored holes through me, challenging me.

We broke camp, threw our things into the truck, and tore down the mountain to get Dena to a hospital, her finger wrapped in a cold wet cloth. Deadly silence settled on all of us the entire trip.

We got her home and, in various states of shock, we went our separate ways. No one spoke about it again. Part of me agonized over how to help Dena. I waffled between rage and empathy, between fear and sympathy. Emotions collided for weeks.

Then Dena finally broke the silence and called. She was cheery, upbeat, and thrilled that her finger was like new. She made a crazy joke about the "accident" and ended with, "Let's get together." Part of me bought it, and part of me recoiled. I knew I was in over my head, and I could feel the current dragging me lower and lower.

I did manage to squeak out, "No, I'm pretty busy right now."

Winter arrived. We had occasional phone conversations, mostly one-sided, as I could find very little to talk about; the darkness was creeping into me, too. I struggled through finals and anxiously awaited Christmas break. I dreaded spending Christmas at home because I knew Mom would ask about Dena, and what could I say? Certainly not the truth. I began scheming ways to skirt around it.

As I headed to Windsor to spend the holidays with my family, I thought of Dena having no one. Her mom was dead. Her dad was detached. She had no siblings, no friends. The desire to make her holidays easier hounded me. However, I didn't want her around my younger siblings.

Then Mom jumped in. "Hey, let's invite Dena to come to midnight Mass, stay the night, and open packages with us on Christmas morning."

"Uh, Mom, I'm not sure that's a good idea."

"Well, she has no other friends but you, and I'd love to see her again. Let's call her," Mom chirped and grabbed the phone.

Done deal.

Willies.

Mom asked Dena to come for dinner at 5:00, but she declined and arrived much later, about 11:00. Mom hurried to hug her while I just nodded and remained seated.

"I'm so excited to join you all at church," Dena bubbled. "I've never been to a Mass, but it must be a very special time. Shouldn't we get going to make sure we get a seat? You know it'll be crowded. A lot of people go to church once a year on Christmas. What a great spiritual time for church people." She chattered on and on, and Mom drank in every word.

This is not Dena, I thought. Effusive. Talkative. Too excited. Too much. Something askew. Something very crooked. Dread replaced the willies.

"Okay! Kathy, you come with me. Marty, we'll follow," ordered Dena.

"Well, I don't thin…"

"Great idea, Dena! We'll see you there," Mom agreed, cutting me off.

Done deal.

Dread inched toward terror.

Dena headed to the bathroom and stayed just long enough for my family to pull away from the house.

"Okay. Let's go *now*."

My breath caught at the "now." She had planned not to follow them.

"Okay," I hesitated as she put the car in gear. "Take a left on 7th Street then another left on Walnut. Go about seven blocks, and we're there. The church is on the right side."

Dena flew past 7th, headed out of town, and jerked us onto the first dirt road she came to. Sliding around the corner, barely avoiding the ditch, she flattened the accelerator and raced away from Windsor.

Our Father, who art in heaven…. Help! I'm in trouble. Please help me. Full blown terror, now. My insides trembled. I had met evil in her apartment. Now I was alone with it, in the middle of nowhere.

Without warning, she slammed on the breaks, sending us into violent swings. *We're gonna roll. We're gonna roll! Oh, God, help me! I'm in trouble. Please help me, God!*

We fishtailed to a stop, and her hands clamped onto my forearm. Her fingers dug into my skin. I jerked my head toward Dena. Her blue eyes were blood red, the pupils vertical slivers of black. "I waannnt yooouuu," she growled, or rather "it" growled. Dena had vanished. Black venom had replaced her. I thought my forearm was going to snap like a toothpick. I was praying hard, asking for my life. Whatever I could pull from my Catholic upbringing. Just seeking heaven. Begging for divine intervention.

I turned away from the hideous face and stared at the moon peeking through a wafer of cloud. *Oh, God. If You're listening, I'm in big trouble. Please help me,* I silently begged, imagining Him just beyond that brilliant light.

"I wannnnnt youuuuu." Over and over and over the voice repeated the words. Pain shooting through my arm, I readied myself for it to snap.

Pleading for God's help and protection . . . again and again and again.

Abruptly, He answered! He broke her grip. The hands lifted, Dena came back—blue eyes, a sweet smile. "Let's go to church." And we did.

I found Mom and slipped in beside her, Dena right behind me.

"Where have you been?" Mom whispered.

I simply shook my head and thought, *You have no idea!*

I struggled through Mass. I took the communion bread with profound reverence. I had been rescued. Evil had me in a death grip, and I had been rescued. Oh, how sweet was that communion time. I stuttered through the last song, and we headed out. I hooked my arm through Mom's and walked straight to our car.

"Oh! Kathy! I have a present for you. Wait a minute." Dena left for her car, bringing back a shoebox wrapped in brown paper. I took it from her, she waved good-bye, and then she left.

I slipped into the backseat, shaken and terrified yet overflowing with thanksgiving. We all went straight to bed, and I'm sure my family slept. I didn't. The brown box haunted me.

Morning came. We opened presents—all but one. We laughed. We had a wonderful Christmas dinner. Then I excused myself and drove to the bluffs west of Windsor to open the brown present. I parked facing the mountains, feeling somehow that I would need divine help again. Beneath my shaking fingers, the brown paper gave way. I opened the box, peeked in, and crushed the box shut! "Oh, God! Oh, God!" I screamed into the heavens above the snowcapped peaks, searching for Him.

I jammed the horrid box under the passenger seat and headed back. In short order, I said my good-byes, gave my hugs, and told Mom I needed to get home to work on assignments.

My heart pounded all the way home. The box seemed to growl and hiss. Those blood-red eyes still stared through me.

Safely home, I called my cousin, Pat. She had lived with us for several years and was really more of a sister than a cousin. She had gotten "saved" and left the Catholic Church, so my family had kind of disowned her. Now I certainly didn't understand getting saved or being born again, as Pat had explained it, but I had met evil, and I knew at least something about devilish power. So whatever spirituality Pat had found, I wanted it.

I could hardly bear to touch the box, but I brought it into the house, dropped it, and then ran for the phone. In breathless, trembling spurts, I told Pat what had happened and that I knew I needed help.

"Kathy, tell me what's in the box."

"Ohhh, Pat, I can't. I cannn't!"

We talked on, and Pat gently walked me through the demonic maze. She prayed with me in phrases I'd never heard—something about being covered by the blood of Jesus and something about greater is He who is in us than he who is in the world—whatever. I didn't get it, but I had to have it. Her faith and knowledge of the Lord Jesus coaxed me to continue.

"It's a wooden doll . . . about nine inches tall. Its hands . . ." I sucked in air, trying to keep breathing, ". . . its hands are tied behind its back. Fingers are missing on each hand . . ." breathing, breathing, ". . . ends painted red and red drops like blood splattered on the back and down the legs. Pat, I cannot do this." I shoved the thing back in the box and crushed the lid over it.

Pat prayed again and shared Scripture with me. She told me about Jesus and His power. She told me how He defeated Satan and death at the cross. How when we give our lives to Him, He takes control. She told me about John 10:10, that Satan comes to steal, kill, and destroy, and that Jesus came to give us life, and life abundantly.

"Kathy, you need to press on. Open the box. Tell me the rest."

"Some of its toes are cut off, too, and painted red. There are needles sticking into . . . into . . ." breathing, breathing, "into one eye, into its knees and neck and back and . . . PAT! I can't do this!"

Pat prayed that the Holy Spirit would cover me and strengthen me. I didn't know a thing about the Holy Spirit stuff, but she did.

"Kathy, God is three persons in one. There is God the Father and God the Son and God the Holy Spirit. He comes to live in us when we give our lives to Jesus as Lord. He empowers us to do what we can't do on our own."

I knew nothing about the Holy Spirit. We only said His name when we made the sign of the cross.

"The needles. . . ." I had to finish telling Pat about the needles —with blood dripping from each one. I told her about the eyes. The same blood-red eyes with slivers of black that shot pure hate through me in that car on that remote dirt road. I told her about the tangled, bloody hair and the needles sticking out of the head. I told her everything. She prayed again and slowly explained what to do about it.

"Kats, you must burn it. Stay on the phone. Take it, the paper, and the box. Take extra paper, some small wood that you use in your outdoor grill, and burn it."

While I carried out each step, Pat prayed protection over me. Prayed about me being covered by His blood. I knew I had to ask her about that when this was all over. At the time, blood was the *last* thing I wanted to think about.

It burned and burned and burned. The phone went dead. I ran into the house, put it in its cradle to charge, and kept adding more and more wood. The doll still kept burning.

I finally dialed Pat again, "Pat! This can't be happening! This isn't possible! It's been over four hours, and it's still burning." The rancid smell burned my eyes and nose. "This can't be!"

So she schooled me on demonic things, on supernatural things, especially on God's supernatural power, which is greater than Satan's. This was no ordinary three-by-nine-inch wooden doll. It would burn until the battle was won.

The burning stopped about 5:30 that next morning. After charging the phone the fourth time, I called Pat. She praised God like I'd never heard anyone do before, and we hung up. I pondered the things Pat had told me—the things about God and Jesus and the Holy Spirit; about being born again; about God's power. My rigid muscles began to relax. The horror of it all loosened its grip.

The phone rang, jerking me out of the first peace I'd felt in months. *Who'd be calling at this hour!*

"Youuuu burrrrrned *it!*" the voice growled and hissed and hung up.

I never heard from Dena again.

The Almighty God, whom I didn't even really know, had kept me from evil. Peter says it this way: We are *kept* by the power of God. The root word rendered *kept* in English is priceless and powerful. It means a watcher in advance; that is, to mount a guard as a sentinel or post spies at gates; to hem in, to protect.

Kept by the power of God. I lived the truth of that verse in my demonic encounter with Dena. He kept me then and will never stop keeping me. Oh, how great is the power and love of God.

"KEPT!" – FOR DEEPER THOUGHT . . .

1. Have you ever thought about the spiritual realm all around you, just beyond your sight? What thoughts come to mind right now?

2. In John 10:10–11, Jesus says, *"The thief comes only to steal and kill and destroy; I came that they may have life, and have it abundantly. I am the good shepherd; the good shepherd lays down His life for the sheep."* Jesus died on the cross to save us from our sins and give us abundant life. The devil and his evil forces come to steal, kill, and destroy. Which spiritual force has the most influence over your life right now? Explain.

3. Ephesians 6:10–12 adds this, *"Finally, be strong in the Lord and in the strength of His might. Put on the full armor of God, so that you will be able to stand firm against the schemes of the devil. For our struggle is not against flesh and blood, but against the ruler, against the powers, against the world forces of this darkness, against the spiritual forces of wickedness in the heavenly places."* What schemes of the devil or forces of wickedness have tried to ruin you or may be after you right now?

4. Though these evil forces are real and strong, God's love and power are infinitely stronger. Romans 8:38–39 says it this way: *"For I am convinced that neither death, nor life, nor angels, nor principalities, nor things present, nor things to come, nor powers, nor height, nor depth, nor any other created thing, will be able to separate us from the love of God, which is in Christ Jesus our Lord."* Have you accepted God's almighty love by giving your life to Jesus? If so, how does this verse encourage you? If not, what is holding you back?

5. *"Beloved, do not believe every spirit, but test the spirits to see whether they are from God, because many false prophets have gone out into the world. By this you know the Spirit of God: every spirit that confesses that Jesus Christ has come in the flesh is from God; and every spirit that does not confess Jesus is not from God; this is the spirit of the antichrist, of which you have heard that it is coming, and now it is already in the world. You are from God, little children, and have overcome them; because greater is He who is in you than he who is in the world"* (1 John 4:1-4). What do you learn from this passage? How does it encourage you?

Kept!

No weapon formed can prosper against me.
I am the Lord's.
And I'm kept by the power of God—
Yes, kept by the power of God.
(1 Peter 1:5)

Seriously?

My "life plan" was pretty well set as I approached my twenty-seventh birthday. The encounters with evil seven years earlier were all but forgotten. Now I had a great job, money, and a relationship that would last forever. In fact, we were making plans to buy a home and horses.

I left work early and eagerly headed home and into our future together only to find my partner with someone else. This was the third lesbian relationship I had been involved in and just knew it would be my last. But now this. I was devastated. Crazy with hurt, I bolted to my car and recklessly drove two tanks of gas empty. Screaming and speeding, I swerved from lane to lane, blinded by red-hot tears.

Leaving I-25 and heading into Windsor . . . an 18-wheeler slowed me to a crawl . . . furious . . . stomping on the accelerator . . . flying around the truck, swiping tears away . . . suddenly . . .

nothing but headlights . . . hitting the steep descent into Windsor . . . the semi picking up speed, keeping me from returning to my lane. Seconds to live . . . screaming "Jesus!" . . . jerking the steering wheel . . . clamping my eyes shut . . . waiting to career over the steep drop-off . . . waiting to die. Blackness . . . nothing by blackness.

"Kathy. Kathy." Someone was calling me and patting my cheeks. "Kathy! Wake up." More patting my cheeks. "Kathy. Come on. Talk to me."

I felt as if someone were trying to pull me out of deep water. Things were in super slow motion, happening one still frame after another after another.

"Kathy."

My eyes slowly opened.

"Oh, good," Mom exclaimed. "You're back!" There I sat at the kitchen table in my folks' house, four miles from Windsor hill. "Kathy?" Mom whispered.

I'm dreaming or dead, I thought but said nothing.

"Kathy, what's going on?" Mom scooted her chair closer, bumping my chair, forcing some kind of response.

"How d-did I g-get here?"

Wrinkles furrowed Mom's brow as she was trying as hard as I was to piece together what had just happened.

"You—you drove. Your car is . . . is in the driveway," she stammered.

Silence.

"You've been crying," she coaxed.

"Oh, yeah," I began. "Debbie said something that hurt, but I'm okay. Really. I'm okay. It's no big deal."

"Well, how about a cup of tea and a piece of your birthday cake?" she offered.

"No. Thanks. I want to go downstairs and lie down for a bit," I replied evenly, because I could see that she was worried. A strange numbness and emptiness had settled over me. We were like two wooden puppets, facing each other, dangling from strings—on a barren stage.

I headed for the basement bedroom that I had chosen many years prior. My folks had moved to Windsor when I was seventeen, but I had stayed in Denver to finish high school and two years at Metro State College. When I did finally move north to work for Kodak, I lived with my folks for a year, and that isolated bedroom was perfect. Cool in the summer. Quiet. Dark. When opportunities arose to sleep in, I was completely delighted with the darkness. Now that darkness drew me deeper.

I closed the door and sank onto my bed, the numbness swallowing me. Memories of my brother drifted in and out of the darkness and across my mind. He was twelve, I was ten, and we were inseparable. A drunk driver had taken his life, and in so many ways, mine, as well. Then the encounter with Teri after being paired with her for a Language Arts project in my first year of high school surfaced in the darkness. Quite unintentionally one day, I had mentioned something about my brother, Eddy, and she had asked about him. I had not spoken a word about this deep wound since his death—his name had been forbidden in our house. As Teri asked more and more questions, the wound split open and pain surged out. I emptied the details of his horrific accident for the first time. We hugged, and in a very short time Teri led me into lesbianism. Those memories still shocked and shamed me. My secret wound had been opened and now felt infected. As I lay there in the cool darkness of my room, the desperation and pressure of those memories held me captive. Over the years since that first encounter with Teri, I had become convinced that I was born gay and had stopped resisting. In fact, I had put my entire heart and soul into this third relationship with Debbie and now this. As I lay there, it became clear that this would be my last—if not one way, then another.

Into the darkness came the image of an X-ACTO® knife in my desk drawer. I got up and quickly found it. I fell to my knees and decided. No hysteria. No angst. No reason to live.

I can't make it in the lifestyle, but I can't seem to get out. This is my only choice. Empty and now completely numb, I pressed the razor-sharp blade into my left wrist.

"Knock, knock. Hey, Kathy, it's Cousin Pat. Happy Birthday!"

I kept pressing the blade. Mindless. Deaf.

"Hey, let me in," Pat said, forcing the door open.

Shocked by the horrifying scene, she grabbed the knife, threw her arms around me, and held me hard. She rocked me. She prayed for me. And rocked me and prayed for me. She held me and pressed me to her and loved me to life.

What a wild intervention. We hadn't seen Pat for many years, and I hadn't talked with her much since she saved me from Dena's evil seven years ago. I mean, we were Catholic after all, and Pat had left the Church years before. She became a Protestant and was "born again," which meant that "good" Catholics like us shouldn't have anything to do with her. I didn't get it, but it's the way it was even though we loved and missed her.

Pat had been an integral part of our family years earlier. She moved in with us when I was nine and she was fifteen and soon became our favorite cousin. When my older brother was killed, Pat had held things together for us. She mothered me, my two sisters, and my little brother. She kept things sane as our lives whirled out of control. She withstood Dad's drinking and the abusive behavior. She loved us, and we loved her. She was a vital part of our family for five years . . . until she married.

Now, she just *happened* to show up, in the late evening, for my birthday?

Seriously?

She bandaged my wrist, cleaned up the mess, and tucked me into bed like she did when I was little. "Can I pray for you?" she asked.

"Whatever." It didn't matter to me one way or the other. I didn't want to live, and Pat had made sure I would. I wasn't happy about that.

Pat prayed on and on in an unintelligible language. I tuned out the gibberish, but I couldn't ignore what was happening inside. She had laid her hands on my head, and as she prayed, something like a current of warm water ran from her hands, into my head, down to my toes and back up, over and over—as if I was having a warm, internal bath. I loved it even though I didn't understand it.

"Kathy, if you give your life to Jesus, He'll turn all of this for good," she claimed.

"Whatever," I sighed.

Pat left me lovingly tucked in, and I slipped into a deep sleep until the early morning hours. Then the horrible reality that I was still alive overtook me. Oh, how I wished it weren't true. Just as the familiar desperation began choking me again, I remembered that warm bath when Pat prayed for me. I remembered what she said about giving my life to Jesus and how He would turn it all for good. So, in the silence of that early morning, I whispered, "Jesus, if You are *real*, would You please take my next breath and my next breath and my next breath because I don't want to live. My life is yours." Instantly, a profound peace settled on me, and I knew the Lord was already at work. Sweet sleep followed.

The phone woke me at about 8:00 a.m. and I heard Mom hollering, "It's for you, Kathy."

For me? I had been cut off from every person I knew. *Who'd be calling me?* I wondered and stumbled to the phone, the long sleeves of my jammies hiding the pressure bandage.

It was Karen, an acquaintance from so many years back that I couldn't even remember how we met. How on earth did she even have my phone number?

"Hey, what are you doing this summer?" she asked.

"As of yesterday, absolutely nothing. I have zero plans," I answered. *Is this my first "God working things for good" experience? If my life is His to direct now, and if He had Karen show up out of nowhere after so many years, then so be it.*

"Well, let's go get summer camp jobs."

Karen? For a whole summer? *Seriously?* I couldn't even spend ten or fifteen minutes with her in the past because she drove me nuts. What an insane suggestion from out of the blue, but I had no resolve to say no. Here was this lovable fruitcake back in my life just when all my friends had deserted me.

"Okay," I answered, humbled by God's surprising ways.

"Great! I'll pick you up in two hours," Karen chirped. Her fruity enthusiasm was somehow okay now, even welcome.

She honked; we hugged and headed out. While catching up, I paid no attention to the route, until she stopped in front of the Boy Scout office in Greeley.

"Karen, what are we doing here?"

"Getting summer camp jobs," she hollered, slamming the door and heading toward the entrance.

Crazy, but whatever, I thought. It didn't matter one way or another to me. I was alive, but I had no plans or goals or ideas. I was breathing because God was taking my next breath, and I had no thought beyond that. My life was His, *if* He chose to give me breath. So, how I spent my minutes was His to direct, and He was probably the only one who could get two women jobs at a Boy Scout camp.

A very kind, white-headed man named Stephen welcomed us with a puzzled smile. "Uh, may I help you?"

Karen piped up instantly, "Yes, you can. We want you to hire us to work at the Ben Delatour Boy Scout Ranch this summer."

Poor man. He about choked. He stuttered and squirmed and looked everywhere except at us. I felt for him. I knew the request was bizarre and *so* Karen.

"We, um, we have never hired a . . . woman," he apologized. "I mean, we do have one job open, but, I mean, a woman couldn't, well, a woman can't . . ."

"Tell us what the job is," Karen interrupted. "I bet we can do it." I then remembered why we had only been acquaintances and not good friends. She was not only odd; she was pretty pushy, too. I turned to leave, wanting to give the dear man a break.

"Well," Stephen tried again, still squirming, "it's teaching rifle and shotgun to Scouts who need to earn their firearms badge."

That silenced Karen, perhaps for the first time in years, but it opened my mouth.

"Sir, I have my distinguished medal," I stated flatly.

Poor man. His mouth dropped open and his eyes bulged. "Th-that's the highest medal in the Armed Forces," he stammered.

"I know. It's pretty weird. I shot for the ROTC team in high school."

He paused and just stared. When he finally found his voice again, he asked me about my best aggregate score.

"Three hundred and ninety-eight, sir. I missed two points in the standing position."

Karen squealed, "You shoot? And you shoot almost perfectly? Who knew?"

"Three hundred and ninety-eight!" Stephen repeated, incredulous. "You're hired, but we can't have just one female there, so I'll hire both of you."

"Thank you, sir. Thank you," we answered, knowing he'd be telling this story to all his buddies the first chance he got.

It had been less than twelve hours since my suicide attempt, and God was already proving Himself faithful. I thought back to yelling out, "Jesus" and jerking my steering wheel over the edge of the road expecting to die but ending up at the kitchen table instead. I began to realize that only God can do this kind of miraculous stuff, and that He *delights* in doing it—even for someone mired in sin. Maybe *especially* for someone mired in sin.

Still rather numb and not quite so heartbroken, I watched to see what He would do next. He had brought me this far, and if He had more for me, *He* would have to accomplish it as all *my* dreams were dead.

A whirlwind followed. Karen and I headed home, threw a few things in suitcases, and immediately drove to Ogden, Utah, for a week of NRA certification. Mark, the camp director, welcomed us, showed us to our rooms, and said, "Dinner is at 7:00."

That afternoon, I wandered into the woods, pouring my grief out to a Savior I barely knew. I felt lost and so very alone. However, I was alive, and I had no doubt that God had sent

Pat. I remembered the warmth that coursed through my body when she prayed. Dropping to my knees next to a tiny thread of water winding its way to a small pond below, I whispered, "Lord, I don't feel like living, but my life is now in Your hands. Would You please help me find a reason to go on?"

With the afternoon slipping away, I returned to camp. Karen and I shared a simple meal with Mark and listened as he gave a quick rundown of the week's activities.

"You know, you are the first woman to shoot here, so tomorrow morning before breakfast, we'll head to the range and shoot targets before the other instructors arrive."

I nodded, thanked him for dinner, and headed to my room. It took just minutes to snuggle under the thick, warm comforter. *From wanting to die in Windsor, Colorado, to shooting targets in Ogden, Utah.* "What a strange ride You have me on, Lord," I whispered. I didn't even try to understand why He was leading this way, and I had no clue where it would end up. I was very content to simply do the next thing—meet Mark in the morning and shoot targets.

Just as the birds began singing, we headed down toward the pond, Karen chattering like a chipmunk all the way. It didn't take a genius to figure out what Mark was doing. He wanted to have proof for the twenty-nine men arriving the next morning that I was qualified to be there. Whatever. I had no axe to grind. I set up my first target and relaxed into the prone position. Mark helped me sight my rifle in, and I lost myself in the moment.

That's why I loved shooting. I could shut out the world—my brother's death, my dad's abuse, my own shame, and whatever else each day might throw at me. Shooting was what had gotten me through high school.

I drew in a deep breath, exhaled, and squeezed off the first round. Mark totaled my four targets: prone, sitting, kneeling, and standing.

"I'll just hand these to the first complainer," he quipped and winked. *Thank You, Lord, for Mark,* I thought as we headed back to the lodge.

Throughout the morning, male Scout leaders from all over the country arrived to get certified. Many of them were not pleased that Karen and I were there, and all of them but one took offense that I'd been hired to teach rifle and shotgun. The Eagle Scout leaders were particularly angry that their boys would be taught by a woman.

That instigated quite a week. But I had a secret weapon—Karen! All of her quirks that drove me crazy in the past were just the ticket with these stuffy leaders, and Mark unabashedly egged her on. She conveyed a hilarity and joy that was quite foreign to me and, to my amazement, quite healing.

"Come on, Kathy. We're getting our uniforms!" she yelled and dragged me toward the lobby. She bounced right into the midst of the leaders, shouting "I'm a Boy Scout now," and then she struck a pose that made many of the leaders laugh, Mark slapping high fives all around.

In our official uniforms now, the next activity was to meet at the range. Karen watched while the rest of us reviewed the rules about safety, cleaning weapons, ammunition, and how to manage a range with boys from Cub Scouts to Eagle Scouts.

Mark watched and listened carefully. When we were just about ready to break for dinner, he stopped class to make a surprising announcement.

"I think it's time for Kathy and Bruce to grab a couple rifles and show us how it's done. Check the target distance and your weapons, count your ammunition, choose someone to help you sight-in, and let's shoot four targets," he instructed and winked at me.

Karen shot me a terrified look. I grinned back and settled into the prone position. Pressure? Absolutely none. There was nothing to prove. The Lord had seen me through thus far, and a calm assurance made me think He would see me through this moment, too. He hadn't intervened in my suicide attempt to forsake me now.

I finished a bit before Bruce, handed my targets to Mark to score, and Karen and I headed back to the lodge. The guys streamed in behind Bruce, who gave me a high five. Karen beamed like a proud parent with a successful kid. I smiled because God is good, and Mark had ingeniously and graciously "won" Bruce, the stuffiest leader, over. Now we were accepted and even appreciated.

Over the next six days, one of us would act as instructor, trying to manage eight other simulating rambunctious Scouts. We laughed and joked. We scolded and kicked some off the range for serious infractions. We tested our instructors, knowing that kids and guns are a serious thing and that we needed to be ready for anything. Respect and order had to rule the range, while at the same time giving the Scouts a positive experience as they worked toward their badges. Their very lives would be in our hands.

We instructors spent the last day playing all kinds of games in teams of four, Bruce and I on the same team. What a sweet, amazing week. Laughter returned to my life, and my awareness of the Lord's presence heightened daily.

When the instructor orientation was over, we went home, repacked, and headed straight to the Ben Delatour camp, west of Ft. Collins. We had three days to prepare for the arrival of four hundred Boy Scouts. After settling into our little cabin, we walked to our worksites to prepare. Karen had been hired to help with crafts, and I had weapons to clean, inspect, and fire.

Sitting at the range with dozens of weapons and countless ammunition, I laughed out loud. *"Lord, seriously?! I'm still pretty heartbroken and fragile. How can I be trusted here?"*

Instantly, I sensed His answer: *Trust Me, not yourself.*
I sat in silence awhile, wondering about what just happened. Months later, I would read what the Apostle John wrote about God's sheep knowing the Good Shepherd's voice and how He knows ours. My simple question on the range that first day and His answer birthed what would become a lifetime of conversation with the Lord. While I was still marveling at His interaction with me and the power of His presence, Karen popped in to check on me.

"Hey, you need this. Read, read, read," she said and handed me a Bible. Catch ya later, okay?"

"Okay. Thanks," I replied. I knew bits and pieces about things in the Bible, but I was hungry to know everything about this God who saved me, guided me to this place, and who had just answered my first question.

As Karen jogged away, I cradled my first Bible. I had been taught that only the priests should use the Bible because lay people couldn't understand it. My family had one on an end table by the couch, but we certainly never opened it. And here I was, broken but alive, a one-week-old baby Christian, beginning to walk with this amazing Jesus, holding my first Bible. I was breathless at the possibilities, even though loneliness still dogged me. Knowing nothing about which books were where or how to begin, I simply asked the Lord to speak to me. Since He just had, I figured He would again. I pressed the Bible shut, then took my hands away and let it fall open wherever, reading the first line I saw.

"The LORD is near to the brokenhearted and saves those who are crushed in spirit" (Psalm 34:18).

"Oh, Lord, that's me," I whispered to Him, somehow knowing that it was no accident that the Bible fell open to that page—that verse. Truly, He was speaking to me again, assuring me that He was right here at the rifle range, that He was with me . . . that I wasn't alone. Yes, my heart was still broken. Yes, the loss of Debbie had crushed me. But He was near.

I scribbled that verse on a piece of paper and put it in my back pocket. It was a life-giving promise that I would feed on all summer. "Okay, Lord. That's that." My reservations about spending the next months with so many Boy Scouts and so many weapons vanished.

The Lord and I spent the rest of the day together cleaning and testing weapons and visiting about that verse. I poured out my hurt to Him, telling Him all about my three relationships, my sin and shame, my inability to change, my sorrow at having turned from what I knew as a child. He reminded me of the warm bath I felt when Pat prayed for me that night. He whispered into my baby spirit that I was clean in Him. Oh, the sweetness of that first day. I was deep in the beauty of the Rocky Mountains and busy digging into the truth of the Word—with Jesus teaching me all along the way.

My three months at Ben Delatour flew by. The pages of that first Bible became wrinkled, dog-eared, and a little dirty with the grime of a rifle range. I had been in charge of my life for twenty-seven years, ruining it, and having a brush with death. Jesus had been in charge for three exhilarating months, restoring laughter and hope and filling me with His life.

To know Jesus as Savior is wonderful. His death on the cross saves those who believe in Him from the penalty of sin and from death. To know Him as Lord, certain that He is in charge, leads to a life of anticipation and wonder.

I left Ben Delatour a different woman—no longer alone, no longer crushed. I left hand-in-hand with my Lord and couldn't begin to imagine what He would do next. Yes, some hurt still lingered, but the Lord had loved me back to life by bringing Karen to walk me through those precious months.

The Gospel of John says, "The thief comes only to steal and kill and destroy; I came that they may have life, and have it abundantly" (John 10:10). I had lived with the devil's schemes for years, but at camp that summer I tasted the sweetness of Jesus's abundance.

Seriously!

"SERIOUSLY?" – FOR DEEPER THOUGHT . . .

1. Has something in your life ever driven you toward discouragement or despair? To whom or what did you turn? What were the results?

2. Have you ever felt that God is very far away or not interested in what's going on in your life? To whom or what did you turn? What were the results?

3. "The LORD is near to the brokenhearted and saves those who are crushed in spirit" (Psalm 34:18). "I will instruct you and teach you in the way which you should go; I will counsel you with My eye upon you" (Psalms 32:8). Knowing this kind of intimate care and guidance is available from the Lord, what could you do and expect the next time a difficult situation arises?

4. How would your life and situation change if you asked Jesus to take the reins of your life? If you have surrendered your life to Jesus, how has He gotten you through hard times?

5. The Bible addresses separation in Romans 8, where Paul asks who or what will separate us from the love of Christ: tribulation, distress, persecution, famine, nakedness, peril, sword, or death? Verses 37–39 give the answer. "But in all these things we overwhelmingly conquer through Him who loved us. For I am convinced that neither death, nor life, nor angels, nor principalities, nor things present, nor things to come, nor powers, nor height, nor depth, nor any other created thing, will be able to separate us from the love of God, which is in Christ Jesus our Lord." How does this truth alter your thinking, especially when you feel separated from God or are reeling in the midst of a difficult situation?

6. How has the Lord met and encouraged you when circumstances overwhelmed you? How has He loved and guided you in the past? Hebrews 13:8 declares, "Jesus Christ is the same yesterday and today and forever." What thoughts come to mind while reading this verse? What can you count on in your present trial or in whatever trial may come in the future?

Seriously?

I am at work . . . working everything
for your good.
I am at work . . . making sure things
turn out as they should.
So child, will you trust Me now, will you slip
your hand into Mine?
And child, will you look My way, and on this
altar will you stay and trust me?
(Romans 8:28)

Black Heart

Today was our first session, and I was actually sort of forced to see Don and Billy. I didn't even know them, but my friend said they were a loving elderly couple who were very active in their church. In addition to their work with other ministries, they volunteered as counselors. They had no degrees, but they had hearts full of compassion, faith that moved mountains, and discernment that could see the unseen. I guess when I bolted off the couch one evening and started screaming obscenities at a TV show, my friend saw that I needed help and made the call.

"I—I'm sorry. What did you ask me?" I stuttered, staring at Don, wrestling my attention back to the present. My mind had wandered back to a dark time in my life, and I felt disoriented and vulnerable.

"Well, you mentioned you *had* a brother. We'd like you to tell us about him."

"No. That's not why I came. I came because I want out of the gay lifestyle. I need you to help me get rid of my homosexual tendencies," I snapped. "I don't need to talk about my brother. That happened a long time ago. It's no big deal."

I followed Don's eyes as he sent a silent message to his wife, Billy. She looked at me and then *through* me. Tears filled her warm amber eyes. Neither of them said anything, and the silence ate at me like coarse sandpaper on soft wood.

I don't need this! I shot up and out of the overstuffed chair and headed for the door, confident that my lifestyle retort would bring them to a relieved "Good-bye."

"Wait. Kathy. Please wait," Billy urged. "I think the Holy Spirit just gave me something, and you will know if it resonates as truth for you or not. Please. You came for help, and we know that God knows exactly what you need."

She had me. I mean, what could I say to that? I stood there— hand on the door—ready to flee.

"Please, Kathy, stay," Don added, his deep brown eyes drawing me, pleading with me to give them, and God, a chance.

I hadn't met Christians quite like Don and Billy before. Genuine. Authentic. I felt their concern and their acceptance without a hint of judgment or condemnation.

After all, I had come for help. Hadn't I? But what if Don and Billy couldn't be trusted? What if God couldn't be trusted? What if my protective walls crumbled? How would I face the pain there?

I glanced back at these two and wondered if they could see this internal war. Their eyes held mine. Tiny tears tracked down Billy's wrinkled face. This little woman and her husband waited . . . silently . . . patiently . . . for my decision.

I really had come for help.

I released the doorknob and slowly slid back into my chair. Don reached out his hands, one to Billy and one to me. They were large, leathery hands. Calloused. Gently strong. I timidly placed my hand in his, and as he wrapped his long fingers around mine, a totally foreign sensation enveloped me. Fear fled, and strange, strong emotions began bubbling up as tears fell onto our hands.

Billy's tears mixed with mine. Healing tears—all mixed together—bathed and washed me. Don's large hands spoke protection, strength, and safety. Time stood still. It felt so foreign, all of it way beyond my understanding. But it was a sweetness I had never tasted. We lingered for a long time like that—three people united by an unseen presence.

"Lord," Don eventually prayed, "have *Your* way here. Please, have *Your* way. Amen."

Bill cupped my hands in hers and looked at me, little pools of tears still hanging in the wrinkled pockets below her eyes. She spoke slowly, cautiously measuring my response with every word.

"We know . . . that this may be new for you . . . and scary . . . but we trust the Holy Spirit to lead us. Sometimes He gives me pictures. *I* don't always know what they mean, but *you* will know if this one is for you or not. So, let's trust God to show us what it may mean. Okay? Are you okay, Kathy?"

"Yeah," I answered quietly, a fragile willingness settling somewhere between my *"I don't need this"* and *"I really did come for help."*

As her eyes held mine, they filled with hurt. I could see it. I could feel it. "Kathy, I saw a heart. It was totally black except for one little spot of pink."

I yanked my hands back and shot hot words at her. "Well, that's easy. It's my sin. It's my years in and out of gay bars and gay relationships. It's my drinking. It's my turning away from my family. Nothing mysterious about that picture," I spat, actually chiding myself, not Billy, with my hateful words.

She listened carefully but slowly shook her head to match Don's words.

"No, I don't think so," Don added. "I don't think it's about sin, Kathy. It's about hurt . . . and pain. Years of deep sorrows, sorrows that have taken life, that have stolen from you, sorrows that have killed parts of you."

His words hit my heart hard, jerking unwilling sobs out of me. I didn't like feeling so vulnerable, but I couldn't control it. So I took a deep breath and let the tears spill. *I guess truth does that.*

Folding her loving hands around mine again, Billy whispered, "Kathy, tell us about your brother."

"Well, he . . . he wa-was my h-hero," I stuttered, flinging tears away with my finger. "He was my world."

"Was?" Don questioned.

"Yeah," I answered, ignoring his emphasis on the past tense. "I was a tomboy from the womb, I think, and could throw a ball before I could walk. We played sports together. We rode bikes together. We got into scrapes together. Eddy would even pay me to play with him instead of practicing the piano.

"We worked together—mowing and trimming lawns in the summer, shoveling sidewalks all winter. He did most of the work but always gave me half the money and acted as if he couldn't have done it without me. It's kind of funny, actually. He just always made me feel so important, like he really needed me, like his world revolved around me.

"He even made money off his teammates by betting on me. 'I bet my little sister can out-throw all of you,' he'd brag. Of course, thriving on his belief in me, I out-threw them every time, practically tearing my arm out of socket at times, but I wasn't going to disappoint my big brother. I was proud of him, and he was proud of me. He was my world. I guess I was his world, too. But that was a long time ago." I abruptly stopped talking and took a deep breath. Don and Billy exchanged glances while I took a peek at the clock.

"Well, let's meet again, next week. Okay?" Billy asked.

"Sure. Thanks," I replied. We hugged, and I left.

The next few weeks passed quickly, uneventfully. I gave little thought to that first meeting. Our weekly time together built relationship and trust. This couple continued to touch me and tend my heart, the black part and the little pink spot not yet deadened with hurt.

I told them more things about Eddy and me: About climbing trees and building a tree house in Grandma's back yard; about eating so many green apples that we were sick for two days; about sneaking our little sister out to his room at night and snacking on junk food; about the scrapes we got into and always won—he wouldn't let me lose; about our wild bike trips and skinned knees; about the games we invented; about how he always chose me first. About our world. About our oneness.

I was able to share these stories without being too emotional. We just talked. Actually, sometimes it seemed like a waste of time—mine and theirs. What all this had to do with counseling I had no clue, but they had grown on me, and I looked forward to our visits.

But then one day, something in me snapped. I was with my friend Paula at the vet's office where she was putting her cancer-ridden black lab to sleep. The big guy stood bravely on the unforgiving metal table while the vet shaved a spot and inserted the needle. Then bam! He dropped. Dead. Ninety-three pounds hit that table. Dead. Right there. Crumpling against me. Dead!

Like a worn cable on a suspension bridge—stretched too far, too tight, for too long—something whipped me into churning black waters. Absolute panic raced through my entire system. Memories like snapshots flashed in my head: *Eddy's bloody pajamas. The crumpled bike. Hidden in the black cellar. Sitting on the cement curb of Florida and Federal. Alone—desperately alone. Rocking. Rocking back and forth. Tucked tightly in a small ball. Rocking. Always rocking. The blood-stained pavement. Eddy's blood. The casket. Eddy's casket. His icy hands. White skin.*

Just as I turned to run, the vet opened the door, and we exited. My breath came in jerky spurts. It was a silent trip home, my friend and I both lost in death. Different deaths. The car stopped, and I bolted into the fields—three hundred and fifty acres. I ran and screamed. Ran. And. Screamed. Until I fell exhausted and completely spent. *What is this?! I'm losing my mind! I need help!* I dragged myself to the house and stumbled to the phone. "B-b-ill-ly, I-I-I need to se-see-see you guys."

Wrapped safely in Don's strong arms and in Billy's intense compassion, I told them about my brother in bursts and gasps, not from my head this time. This telling gushed straight out of my ten-year-old heart, where it had hidden all those years. *This* telling came in wild spurts, like pressurized bubbles bursting to the surface. Don and Billy listened and cried. Their tears mixed with mine like a warm, healing balm. Healing me inside.

"I was ten. Eddy was twelve. He delivered papers in Denver. At 3:00 a.m., a drunk driver struck him from behind, hurtling him through space and then to the pavement. Blood and life oozed from him. His coma lasted two weeks. During that time, the family lived in the ICU. But I was left behind and lived wherever I could get close to him—sitting in the dark cellar, clutching his bloody clothes that the paramedics had cut off and stuffed into a brown paper sack—running my small fingers over his crumpled bike, which was laying helplessly next to the grisly, brown sack—sitting on the curb staring at the blood-stained pavement. Rocking . . . tucked in a tight ball, rocking, for hours. That was as close as I could get to Eddy because ten-year-olds weren't allowed at the hospital. I spent those two weeks kneeling on our low oak coffee table just below the living room picture window . . . waiting for anyone with any kind of news, breath by breath, barely sane.

"Then on the fifteenth day, Uncle Joe burst into the house and barked, 'You don't have a big brother anymore.' Not another word was said. Ever. Eddy's name was never spoken. The empty seat at the table haunted us. Stiff silence imprisoned us. No words. No tears. Nothing."

I paused and looked up at Don and Billy, every sentence, every breath lessening the horrible pain of those buried memories. "At his funeral," I quietly continued, "I climbed onto the stool next to his casket. I held his icy cold hand, believing that it was all pretend, that he would never leave me. Reminding him silently that I was his world. That he couldn't leave me. Reminding him that he was my world.

"Weeks, months, years passed, and reality slowly sunk in. Eddy was dead, and, in truth, so was I. I guess that icy coldness had cut its way into the core of my ten-year-old heart," I finished.

Once again, silence fell, but this time it was a soothing silence. A safe silence. No more need to run, to scream. The fury of the pain had been loosed and spent. Its destructive power was finally destroyed.

God had broken the deadly silence after all those years. He had plunged into the blackness where I had buried the pain. Safely tucked out of sight, it had festered and infected every area of my life.

As the three of us sat, basking in the Lord's love, I thought of Mary Magdalene, a sexually immoral woman filled with seven demons and hated by the religious people who thought Jesus should have nothing to do with her. But Jesus had reached into the blackness of her heart, too, forgiving her and bringing freedom. And, oh, how she had loved Him. That same love flooded my heart, and I remembered Don's simple prayer that first meeting. God certainly did "have His way" in the weeks that we spent together.

I left their home much lighter because a deep sorrow had been healed by the Good Shepherd, the lover of my soul. I left strengthened by the faith and love of a humble couple who were wholly available to be used by Him to reach the unreachable.

They weren't offended by my lesbianism and never did address it. Neither did the Lord. He knew that the crippling pain of Eddy's death needed to be released and healed first, leaving my heart "pinker" and stronger to tackle the next "blackness" when the time was right.

Many years passed before I went back to our little house by Florida and Federal. The owners kindly let me wander from room to room and asked me to tell them the story. It seems the realtor had mentioned that a son had died and that the family had moved. I even sat on that same curb, imagining Jesus sitting with me. Different tears fell this time, though— tears of healing and thanksgiving, washing Jesus's feet just as Mary had done. Eddy's death nearly destroyed me, but Jesus intervened and, in perfect love, healed me.

"BLACK HEART" – FOR DEEPER THOUGHT . . .

1. What wound is in your heart that may need attention?

2. Is there anyone you know who would give you biblical advice and pray with you about your pain? Someone you trust and with whom you can be honest about your pain?

3. In Isaiah 61:1, the prophet says this about Jesus:
   "The Spirit of the Lord GOD is upon me,

   Because the LORD has anointed me

   To bring good news to the afflicted;

   He has sent me to bind up the brokenhearted,

   To proclaim liberty to captives and freedom to prisoners."

   In what ways can Jesus be the Answer to your needs?

4. The Lord "heals the brokenhearted and binds up their wounds" (Psalm 147:3). What thoughts come to mind as you read this truth?

5. Sometimes we cause our own pain by making bad choices, and sometimes others cause the pain. Which is it for you, and what steps can you take to forgive yourself or another? Remember, forgiveness often opens the door of healing.

6. "Blessed be the God . . . of all comfort, who comforts us in all our affliction so that we will be able to comfort those who are in any affliction with the comfort with which we ourselves are comforted by God" (2 Corinthians 1:3–4). How does this encourage you? How will you seek God's comfort and then give it to others?

Black Heart

Where do you hide when your heart is breaking?
Where do you run when your tears fall like rain?
Where do you find the strength when
you can't bear the pain?
Go to the Rock
(Psalm 34:18)

Blue Flame

"Welcome to Jewelry 101. My name is Professor Bayt. For tomorrow, read chapters one and two and purchase enough precious metal to begin your first creation. See the addresses on the board. That's it. See you tomorrow."

Well, this sounds easy enough. I think even I can do this, I thought as I exited the building and moseyed toward the campus bookstore, my thoughts wandering here and there.

My move to Windsor had been a good one, and I only needed a few credits to finish the degree I had started in Denver five years prior.

Jewelry 101. My first creation. I liked the sound of that even though the word "creation" didn't fit any fragment of my splintered life. I had trudged through years of destructive behaviors, not creative ones. But I decided to buy some silver and read the two chapters. *Just keep it simple. Don't think past the next concrete thing. Right. Just these two tasks.*

My suicide attempt had jerked me out of my final semester college classes in leaving me with bad grades and an even worse attitude. I spent months bound in hopelessness, but after some counseling, I was tiptoeing back into college, registering for classes that wouldn't strain my tenuous hold on my "new" life. I chose hands-on classes where I could do simple, tangible tasks. This was not the time for Philosophy 420 or Literary Criticism. No ethereal meanderings. No analytical thinking. I looked for "safe" classes to help my GPA recover, along with my own fragile sense of well-being.

The next day in class, Professor Bayt skimmed the first two chapters, introduced us to the overall process of making jewelry, and ended with strong cautions about the dangers involved. Just as class ended, he held up a shiny silver ring that he had made in another class. "Making jewelry is not easy. In fact, it is quite dangerous, but it is fun and rewarding. Read chapters three and four, have your metals ready, and come prepared to engage."

I liked him. He was easygoing and soft spoken but thorough— the perfect teacher in my timid frame of mind. *But come on!* I thought. *Jewelry 101 dangerous?* After all, I had already faced the greatest dangers: myself, my deadly thoughts, my personal demons.

Wednesday rolled around, and with silver in hand I chose a spot toward the back of the room. I had always been a "front-row person" until my emotions began crashing like wild breakers against walls of cold stone. They had forced me to sit near exits for quick escapes. For now at least, a seat in the back still seemed a wise choice. The room was more like a small lab than a classroom. Four wooden stools stood by each of the five tables, or stations. Adjacent to each table was an odd structure, some sort of metal barrel. Professor Bayt highlighted the important items in chapters three and four, closed the book, and looked up, a winsome smile spreading across his face.

"So," he began, "take out some paper and design your first piece."

I froze. I was no artist and hadn't done any creative thinking in years. I had no clue what to put on that paper. *Relax. It's not a big deal. Just take your time. He's a reasonable man.*

As if he had heard my thoughts, Professor Bayt moved toward me.

"Stuck? It's hard to get going sometimes, huh?"

You have no idea! I thought, little tremors beginning to roll up my insides.

"Well, what things do you like? Animals? Art? Nature? The moose earrings you have on are great!"

He noticed them? Well, they are my favorite.

He asked a few more questions, his authenticity gently beginning to dismantle the protective walls that still encased my heart. The trembling stopped. Hesitantly, quietly, I offered him a very short, succinct list. In seconds, he drew a dove, as if in full flight, suspended in the middle of an elegantly shaped earring.

"Perfect," I whispered. "Thank you." He moved on to help other students, and wonder seized me. *A dove in full flight. Prophetic? Maybe. Just maybe there is hope for me.* For so long it felt like my wings had been clipped, my spirit grounded. Now, sitting in Professor Bayt's class looking at the dove he had designed for me, a faint breath of hope eased into that void within, which Jesus had so recently begun to fill. *Yeah, maybe there is hope for me—for freedom and flight.*

"So, who wants to go first?"

Startled, I turned toward the back of the classroom where he stood, grinning. Kind blue eyes twinkling, he held up his newly fashioned ring again as if cajoling us to focus on the result, not the process. He himself had said that it wasn't easy and that there were dangers, but he held up that "end result," silently coaxing the first volunteer forward. He didn't push. He didn't hurry. He simply invited.

I timidly slipped my hand up a bit, confident of him, his design, his heart, and oddly spurred on by that dove—by that hope that flickered deep inside my spirit.

"Good. We have a volunteer. Class, please gather around and we'll begin, slowly, one step at a time."

Good, I thought. *Baby steps. I can do baby steps.* Just then, I remembered the hilarious movie *What About Bob?* and something else came alive. A spark of joy ignited. Surprised by the smile bending my lips, I was actually comfortable in my skin for the first time in a long time. It mattered not that the entire class was watching. I trusted Professor Bayt and what this "dove in full flight" might mean for me.

Prof, as he preferred being called, quickly reviewed the first four chapters, hammering home the dangers of the process. "Now, instead of just hearing about the equipment, we'll begin using it." First, he showed us how to turn a design into a waxen model. Next, pressed into a tight group, we began a thorough inspection of my barrel.

The bottom half was solid cement into which a pipe had been centered and sunk so that it could withstand strong pressure. The top of the pipe was cut about four inches below the top rim of the barrel. A hollow metal rod, about the width of my little finger and about three inches shorter than the barrel's diameter, ran through a funny-looking contraption on top of the pipe so that it could spin freely. One end of this hollow rod was shaped to securely hold a crucible, and just behind it dangled a one-inch metal ring. At the other end sat a tiny cup that would hold my mold, my "end result" if all went well.

"Before we actually use metal," Prof began, "watch carefully how I cock the hollow rod." With both hands, he wound the rod around twice, his forearm muscles flexing with the strain, leaving just enough leeway to slip the ring over a small hook welded onto the barrel. Then POP! He hit the switch and the spring-loaded rod released and flew furiously around and around, making the crucible just a faint blur. We flew too! We jumped back, knocking the people behind us like dominoes in a line. After apologies were made for squashed toes and bumped heads, Prof gave us all a steady stare.

"What happened? What's the danger here?" he pressed.

"Concussions?" a tall kid named Ray blurted out. Hearty laughter totally broke our concentration. My laughter surprised me. I couldn't remember the last time I had laughed.

"That was a good one, Ray," Prof chuckled, gathering us back again. "So, what's *another* danger?"

Our chuckles subsided, and when the ensuing conversation ended, we held a reverent awe for this part of the process. Mishandling the cocking process could break fingers, hands, and even wrists. *What a great teacher. He really "got" us by popping that switch and scaring us. No need to re-teach that lesson.* I was feeling better and better about going first. The more he taught, the more he drew me in. But it was more than that. A quiet hope was stirring inside me—like a delicate flower moving in a soft spring breeze.

"The cocking process," Prof restated, interrupting my thoughts, "can and does break bones. Don't forget that."

Sobered by thoughts of breaking bones, we riveted our attention again on his every move. He dropped a marble-sized piece of silver into the crucible, lit a small torch, and meticulously adjusted the flame.

He looked up, waited until every eye met his stare, and then cautioned, "These next two steps happen in a short second. There's no room for error in either of them. Watch closely. Take note of their dangers." He paused, as if carving those thoughts into our brains. "Notice how I'm holding the torch. Notice where I place the flame on the crucible. Notice the perfect blue color of the flame."

He peeked at us. We all nodded even though we had no clue what "perfect blue" meant or why it mattered.

"When the metal becomes liquid, at the precise instant that the dross bubbles to the top, pull the torch, hit the switch, and stand back." Another pregnant pause to press the information into us.

"Uhhh, dross?" questioned the girl next to me.

"I'm glad you asked," Prof answered. "Dross is the waste product, the impurities, in melted metal. It's usually not visible to the naked eye, but it's there, and it *must* be purged from the metal."

We nodded our heads, and he continued. "The fierce centrifugal force of the spinning rod will hurl the blistering dross that rises to the surface onto the sides of the barrel while throwing the pure metal through the rod and into your mold. Just as the hot metal hits your mold, grab the tongs, pinch the mold, and plop it into the water tray hanging on the barrel, opposite the release switch."

Geeze. No wonder he said it wasn't easy. Maybe I don't want to go first.

But just before I could back out, Prof looked at me and invited me to take his place. I inched to his side and waited for his lead, a tight knot forming in my throat.

"All of you are going to go through the process now. As you tell Kathy what to do next and how to do it and what to watch out for, she will complete each step."

Phew. I'm not alone. We're in this together.

First time. Second time. Seventh time. UGH! That blasted blue flame! It stumped and stopped us time and time again. I felt like throwing the torch out the window, but just at that moment, a delightfully unexpected "gem" became apparent to me. The residual darkness inside of me when Jewelry 101 began had vanished. Through our repeated failures, we were developing the solidarity of a tight team, determined to collectively find and fix the problem. I belonged again. I fit.

Class ended the same way the next two days. One or two team members suggested just giving up and dropping the class. The rest of us quickly huddled around them, convincing them to stay. I had a feeling that Prof knew just when to intervene without interrupting the deeper education that was taking place. This wasn't just about jewelry. This was about life. Patience. Dross. Timing. Endurance. Perseverance. Trials. Overcoming.

And I thought Philosophy would be tough!

The next day, Prof *did* step in and quite forcefully called us into a small circle. "So, what's the problem?" He clearly didn't want even one of us to move toward a barrel and face failure again.

Grumbles and complaints flew freely. "Heck if we know," we all blurted in various ways, a few retorts sharpened with creative cuss words.

The consummate teacher, instead of giving us an answer, he resolutely, yet gently, talked us through the entire process one more time, letting us discover the answer ourselves. "Tell me what pops into your head. Nothing's too dumb to say."

Like popcorn, ideas shot here and there from all of us.

"Perfect blue? When the flame is the hottest?"

"What about the length or the force of the flame?"

"Maybe it's about the angle of the flame?"

"Is it about the pressure of the flame or how close it is to the crucible?"

"Hey! What about when we remove the flame? We're taking it away the instant we see the metal collapse."

"Maybe that's it! Maybe we're removing the heat too soon!"

"Yeah! When the metal collapses, maybe that's not when it is the hottest!"

"Hey! Yeah! It melts but has the dross surfaced? Maybe the dross is still below the surface, so the metal is still too impure or too thick to slide through the rod into the crucible! Maybe it needs *more* blue flame! More torch!"

"Or more *time!*" Randy exclaimed.

"*Bingo!*" Prof shouted, beginning a wave of slapping high fives all around. We all bolted back to our barrels. Our end results were finally within reach. Soon, all of us would have a finished product fashioned with precious metal. And, if we had the eyes to see, we also had something of much deeper value— precious truths with which to fashion fuller lives.

High fives filled the next few classes as each of us finally got to grab the tongs and flip molds into cold water, cheers erupting with every plop and splash. One by one, we held up finished products and then hurried to help others. The teamwork was sweeter and stronger every day. It brought fullness, laughter, compassion, and confidence.

Somehow, I had been caught in a whirlwind of healing grace when all I had hoped for was an A. But Jewelry 101, a great teacher, a simple design, a pair of earrings, and a dangerous process changed me forever. Mysteriously, beyond anything I hoped for or imagined, the class strengthened my resolve to head into the winds of change that the Lord Jesus had begun in my life the night that cousin Pat told me about His great love for me . . . the night she had interrupted my suicide attempt.

Words surfaced in my spirit. *The Lord sits as the refiner and purifier of silver, purging me as gold and silver, forcing my "dross" to surface, refusing to let it remain, then flinging it away, ignoring my fleshly cries for relief, resisting my childish efforts to squirm out from under the blue flame too soon. The nail-scarred hands of the gentle Lord Jesus hold the torch. The perfect refiner sitting intimately involved with the process of creating wonderful "end products."*

Yes. Full flight!

"BLUE FLAME" – FOR DEEPER THOUGHT...

1. How have you failed miserably? Were you afraid to begin again? What did your new beginning look like? Or, if you still need a new beginning, what is the first step?

2. What work do you still need to do to bring that new beginning to maturity?

3. Quietly take inventory of your life. What "dross" resides within you that diminishes your "end results"?

4. The LORD instructed the prophet Jeremiah about the work of the Potter with the clay. It is a clear picture of God's work with us. "But the pot he was shaping from the clay was marred in his hands; so the potter formed it into another pot, shaping it as seemed best to him . . . 'Can I not . . . do with you as this potter does?' declares the LORD. 'Like clay in the hand of the potter, so are you in My hand . . .' (Jeremiah 18:4, 6 NIV). How receptive are you to the Potter and the work He longs to do in you? What might be hindering your receptivity?

5. How can you participate more fully with the Lord's work of removing your dross, that which has spoiled or marred you?

6. "Blue flames" take many forms: sickness, injury, a relationship, a superior, an occupation, a loss, an accident, grief, etc. What is your blue flame right now? How are you embracing it or how are you trying to take it away before it can do its work?

7. Paul writes this in Romans 5:3–5: ". . . we also exult in our tribulations, knowing that tribulation brings about perseverance; and perseverance, proven character; and proven character, hope; and hope does not disappoint, because the love of God has been poured out within our hearts through the Holy Spirit who was given to us." How do these verses encourage you? How is your hope of seeing that "end product" completed?

Blue Flame

My Lord, You are the refiner. My Lord, burn the
dross out of my soul.
Make me gold, oh my God, that I might fear You.
You're the refiner; I yield to You.
(Malachi 3:3)

Let Go

Rarely does a three-year-old or lunch at Burger King radically alter one's life. It's not like I had planned on eavesdropping and soaking up every word from the booth in front of me, nor had I expected a "fast food" lunch stop to last over an hour. It just happened. Like always, I innocently placed my order, slipped into my favorite booth with my lunch, and opened the sports section of the local paper. This routine never took more than fifteen minutes. That is, until today.

I buried myself in the headlines and hardly noticed when a couple and their child settled into the adjacent booth. They talked and ate quietly, and lunch moved along quite normally.

Then, in an instant, the little one hit the volume switch and began bouncing soprano screeches off the walls. Eating stopped. Heads popped up. Employees looked. I stared. The couple squirmed a little, while deepening shades of pink spread over their faces, but they made no move to leave.

Exasperated, I snapped the sports pages shut and started wrapping the rest of my lunch for a quick getaway. I grabbed my Pepsi and began sliding out of my booth when the man's words grabbed my attention like a strong magnet. I settled back in, re-opened the paper for pretense and listened more intently, still annoyed but wanting to stay for some strange reason.

"Laura, honey, just let go," the man whispered.

"NOOOOOO! I want a French fry!" she screamed.

"Honey, if you just let go, you can have more fries," the dad coaxed.

"NOOOO! I want a French fry!" the little one bellowed.

Geez, just give her some fries. What's the big deal? I thought as I snuck a quick peek over the top of my glasses at the little girl, giant tears spilling onto her burger.

"Laura, honey, we have a pile of fries, but you need to let go of the one in your hand before you can take another one," the woman cooed.

Huh? Already has one? So why is she screaming for another one? What's with this? Perhaps by now you have already deduced that I am single and know absolutely nothing about toddlers.

Intrigued by this intense power struggle, I stopped peeking and started watching the three of them. Both of Laura's small, white-knuckled fists were clenched for battle. She occasionally gnawed at the reddened top of one fist, as if she could suck out the mashed mess of a fry.

This could take a while, I thought.

Every wail flooded her round cheeks with crimson and hardened her defiant stance like fast-drying concrete. The couple leaned toward each other and began whispering, discussing strategic tactics I guessed, but there was no retreat in their demeanor.

I began to wager who would win and how long it would take. I hastily placed my bets but had to change them repeatedly as the three continued sparring. I mean, had I been Laura's parent, I would have died of embarrassment and fled at the first wail. Like I said, I know nothing about raising little kids. This was not a skirmish. This was war, and neither side wanted to lose. I admired the resolve of this couple and waited expectantly for their next move.

"Honey, we have a whole pile of French fries. We want to share them," the dad continued as he ooohed and ahhhed about his own tasty lunch, picking up one fry at a time and theatrically lifting each to his mouth, smacking his lips as if he were up for an Emmy.

"Oh, I can hardly wait to eat alllllll of my fries. Theeese are the best French fries I've ever tasted!" mom emphasized.

Aha! I spotted the first signs of surrender. Laura's next few wails lessened in volume and length, and the little girl's eyes began to move up and down, tracking each fry that mom and dad slowly lifted to their mouths. With mom and dad totally immersed in Act 2 of this drama, little Laura looked away from her adversaries and began taking quick peeks at the pile of fries.

Hmmm . . . trying hard to not give in, I guessed. Little by little, color returned to her white knuckles as she loosened her grip.

She's weakening, I whispered to myself as I changed my bet yet again.

And the parents? Geniuses. They just kept talking softly, totally impervious to the ruckus and oblivious to the crowd around them.

Sympathy actually crept into my heart for Laura. She still had no French fries, and now she didn't even have the attention of her parents. *Wow! These guys should have more kids. They're good.*

No more screams. In fact, minutes without a peep multiplied as Laura weighed her options and surveyed her parents.

Very nonchalantly, mom finally spoke. "Hey, Laura, guess what?" as if noticing her for the first time. "If you'll let go of the icky, gooey, cold, squashed fry in your hand, you can have a brand new, warm fry."

Ohhhh, . . . that's good, mom.

I'm captivated now. This was like a graduate-level "child-raising" course. Taught right in the University of Life. For free.

Dad faced Laura now, dramatically lifting an especially long fry to his mouth. "Yum," he declared.

That did it. Trying not to be too obvious about her surrender, Laura opened her tiny fists and quickly scraped out the remains of the first fry. Then, a little suspiciously, she glanced at mom and dad and then at her pile of fries. A tiny smile bent her lips as she chose one and zipped it into her mouth. No clenched fists this time. As she licked and smacked her lips, all three laughed.

"Sometimes you just have to let go," dad said thoughtfully as they all dove into the rest of their lunch with gusto.

The war had ended.

Time moved on, and the little family finished their lunches and left. I, however, didn't budge.

Sometimes you just have to let go.

My heart pounded against my ribs as my mind wrapped itself around the profound truth I had just heard and seen played out before me in living color. It was as if I had been granted a front-row seat at a great theatre where the intensity and passion of the trio in this three act play had rocked my world; had challenged the fear and anger and pride that kept my own fists clenched; had shot doubt into my belief system; had pried my own hands open.

Sometimes you just have to let go. The words echoed back and forth in the quiet caverns of my soul. Slowly, a well-worn story about Jesus and a rich young ruler worked itself into my mind, and I sensed a rumble deep within me. The young man, I think, really wanted to follow the Lord and asked what he should do. Jesus told him to keep the commandments, to which he quickly replied that he had done that since his youth.

Then Jesus uttered the words that shook his world . . . that challenged his clenched fists. Jesus told him to "just let go"—to sell all he had, give it to the poor, and come follow Him. Luke concludes by telling us that the young man turned away full of sorrow.

I resonated with him, with the war being waged in his heart: A war between clutching things and letting go; a battle between independence and surrender; a clash between following whole-heartedly and living lukewarmly.

I don't know how long I sat there, watching various scenes of my life flashing into my memory. Times of loss and hurt. Times when I "iron-gripped" people and things that I couldn't dare lose. Times that I almost squeezed the very life out of what I clutched so desperately. Times of wailing, reddening my own closed fists, hanging on, blind to the entire "pile of fries" in front of me.

Sometimes you just have to let go.

I deliberately, thoughtfully, opened both of my hands, palms up, and laid them on the table. *Lord, may I live with open palms so that You never have to pry my fingers off of anything or anyone.*

I slid out of my booth and shuffled out the door. Unlike the rich young ruler who walked away full of sorrow, I drove away with a lightness, a freedom sweet to the soul, and a warm place in my heart for a tiny stranger named Laura and her wise parents.

"LET GO" – FOR DEEPER THOUGHT . . .

1. Have you ever held someone or something too tightly? How did that work out for you?

2. What's in your fist at present and what stress is it causing you?

3. Letting go can be excruciating, but what do you stand to gain if you do let go?

4. List the reasons that your grip may be too tight. What would be the first step in dealing with these reasons so that you can loosen your grip?

5. As you think about letting go, list the positive, healthy things that could fill that emptiness. Be creative.

6. Paul speaks to letting go in Philippians 3:7–8. "But whatever things were gain to me, those things I have counted as loss for the sake of Christ. More than that, I count all things to be loss in view of the surpassing value of knowing Christ Jesus my Lord, for whom I have suffered the loss of all things, and count them but rubbish so that I may gain Christ." How do these Scriptures challenge you and perhaps help you begin letting go?

7. Hebrews 12:26 says that God will shake not only the earth but also the heaven "yet once more." Verse 27 continues: "This expression, 'Yet once more,' denotes the removing of those things which can be shaken, as of created things, so that those things which cannot be shaken may remain." How does this help you evaluate what you are holding on to? What does it enable you to let go of?

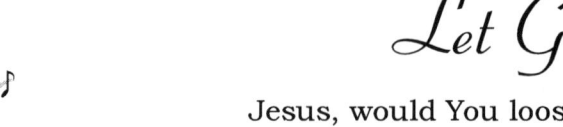

Let Go

Jesus, would You loosen my grip?
Yes, I hold on. Oh, I hold on to things that
damage my soul.
Yes, I hold on. Oh, I hold on when Your
love alone makes me whole.
Oh, by Your grace, I let go.
(Hebrews 12:27)

Idols

"Seventeen hundred dollars! That's a whole lot of money! Money I don't have," I snap as I screw my face into a tight frown. Roy's deep-brown eyes hold mine tightly, as if he is measuring me somehow. "If you're supposed to go, the money will come. Just sign your name and have some faith."

So I scribble my name, turn and head to my car, mumbling as I go. *Yeah, right. Just have some faith. Money doesn't grow on trees! Why on earth did I go ahead and sign up for this crazy trip, anyway?* I jerk my car door open, hit the ignition, and flip the button for my convertible top. It slides open easily, and once in place, I flatten the accelerator, spraying gravel everywhere. *Oh, I love my car!*

But the stubborn facts of how strangely the day has unfolded will not be silenced. Even my best mental gymnastics do not convince me that it is mere coincidence. I mean, what are the chances that I would be at *this* church on *this* day for *this* announcement? After all, I have lived near Roy's church for years and have not attended a single Sunday service until now. But facts are facts. I *did* attend this morning, Roy *did* announce a two-week missions trip into Eastern Europe, my heart *did* jump as he spoke, and I *did* sign up.

As I drove, my mind drifted back to that scene: Upbeat music met me at the door—*strum, strum, sing, sing*—the pastor's youthful zeal and heartfelt message . . . the pastor, suddenly waving for the music to stop and telling us about how Communism had fallen . . . how the doors into Eastern Europe had swung open . . . how their church was sending a mission team there in five weeks . . . "so sign up today and get the details later," he had urged. The service ending . . . people leaving . . . me shuffling forward, signing my name . . . because I simply knew that I had to go on that trip. *Okay. So this can't all be a coincidence. I'm supposed to go. All I need to do is find the $1,700.*

I had been doing all sorts of odd jobs, none of which paid well, certainly not enough to save that much money. Still feeling disgruntled, I toss up a halfhearted prayer, you know, the kind that you're pretty sure will never be heard or answered: "Well, Lord, if *You* want me to go, *You* will need to help with the money. And, Lord, I don't know one person in that church. I don't know why I signed up. I know nothing about Eastern Europe . . ." I continue to fill Him in on all the reasons why the trip doesn't make any common sense, and as I finish my one-sided conversation, I smile at the thought that immediately follows. *When does God ever make sense? If He made sense, He wouldn't be big enough to be God! If He moved me to sign up, then He'll make it work.*

So I just went about my business the next few weeks without thought of Pastor Roy, the trip, or the money. Figuring it was a done deal, I settled back into my usual routine. Whether we really like what we're doing or not, the familiar is comfortable, and I had settled, quite easily, back into the familiar—back to those odd jobs.

I had just finished my bachelor's degree in Physical Education with an emphasis in coaching and a minor in Language Arts but hadn't even tried to look for a position in the school system. Returning to my odd jobs paid the bills and gave me time to recover from the very heavy course load of the past two years.

Then a colleague who had just noticed a job posting at her school called to tell me that she just *knew* I was the teacher for the job. Now, finding middle school teachers is never easy, but finding one seven months into the school year is nearly impossible. And finding one who teaches Language Arts? Well, you'd have better luck getting a toasty warm day in Antarctica.

"Can you interview today?" my friend pleads.

"What?"

"Can you interview today? The principal wants to talk with you *today.*"

"Jan, this is nuts, but I'll be there in an hour."

The "interview" takes four minutes. Dr. Lind glances at my resume, motions for me to follow, and promptly introduces me to my fourth-period students. This sour-looking bunch, pretty hacked that their "real" teacher had resigned, shoot icy glares at me as if that were my fault.

"You'll begin tomorrow morning at 7:30," he hollers over his shoulder as he hustles to his next meeting.

Great, I think to myself as I leave the building. *Four periods of Advanced LA. That's a nightmare. Just grading the papers triples the load. And I start off with angry students. That's like jumping into a swamp of alligators.* Outside I kick a flattened can across the staff parking lot, turn, and march back into the building toward Dr. Lind's office to resign before I even start.

Roy's encouragement to "*just have some faith*" echoes in my heart. I quicken my steps. Just as I enter the front doors, the lunch bell rings, and the little captives explode out of their classrooms. Half head to the lunch room. The rest stampede right toward me for outdoor time. A middle school "lunch rush" is quite a spectacle. The sheer energy would be the fuel source discovery of the century if it could be bottled and sold.

I smile and watch the biggest bunch, mostly boys, head straight for my car. I fly out the doors and scamper after them. "Eww. Tighht! Niiice." High fives to anyone within reach as if they'd just won my car in a contest.

"Is this *your* car?"

My "yes" makes me an instant celebrity. A fresh wave of high fives includes me this time, making my palms sting. They shoot questions at me, and I shoot back answers. They raise and lower the top. They sit in the bucket seats. They touch everything touchable, and most of them even miss lunch.

I am *in*. Oh, the marvel of middle schoolers. They love and hate and hurt and laugh and fly and fall in nanoseconds. Tomorrow's teaching "load" is suddenly looking much lighter. My thoughts of resigning vanish in their spontaneous, lovable rapture over my "hot" car.

Word spreads fast. By the end of the day, anyone who had missed the action had gotten the full scoop from a member of the "in" lunch bunch. I suddenly have a huge fan club—loyal to the bone. They are mine, and they make sure that the newcomers join the group. What that means in the classroom is magic. Sheer magic. It's teaching at its best. It is life-changing and it is reciprocal. Alive. Dynamic. It finds and then floods those deep, seldom-satisfied places in a human heart where perfect contentment plays hide-n-seek, always just out of reach. Well, obviously, I began my teaching job the next morning.

The next two months speed by, every day a full-out sprint just to stay an inch ahead of being buried. I do not even think about the mission trip into Eastern Europe. The last day of school comes and goes with its usual hugs and tears and yearbook signings, quickly pushing the trip to center stage. In fact, we are scheduled to head into Eastern Europe in three weeks.

I know that serving people just freed from decades of Communist rule will more than match the fulfillment of the last two months of teaching. That same "something" that first urged me to sign up for the trip, now insistently beckons me. *I must go. It would be easier and more comfortable to stay, but I must go. Just have some faith.* Roy's words didn't bite anymore. In fact, an odd assurance whispers that the money will come just in time. How? I have no clue because teaching part-time for two months has only paid the bills. It certainly isn't my ticket overseas and the two-week stay.

Once the students are gone, I finish the last of the school duties and head toward my car—the car that had won me my students—the car that always made people stop and stare— the car that I had wanted to own since the day they were made in 1972—my metallic blue, 350 Chevy Super-Sport Malibu Convertible—the car, now a classic, that I have owned for twenty-four years and will keep forever. Newly restored, with headers, air shocks, and a brand new white top.

An idol.

What? Where did that word come from? What do you mean— idol? Yeah, I love this car, but it's not an idol! Yeah, I could sell it, but why would I do a stupid thing like that?

The animated conversation with myself continues. *Of course I can give it up if I have to! But why would I have to? Well, I could. I could . . .*

The next thought stings me.

But will I?

Now, that is a different thing altogether. Defiantly, the question stands before me. What were at first harmless musings about getting rid of my beloved car have somehow turned into a real haunting. *Will I?* My shallow quip of "Of course, I can give up my car" has now become a question of obedience, a question of faith, a question of my willingness to accept God's help when it cuts across the strength of my selfishness and the power of my wants, cuts across releasing the things that matter to me.

"So *this* is how You're gonna help my finances?" I ask as I gaze into the pale-blue sky.

No peace now. In fact, a war is raging between flesh and spirit. *I love lowering that new top, letting the wind whip my hair. I love the pleasant purr of the headers and the power to merge onto a highway in seconds, forever redefining yield signs. I love the looks and the attention that it draws. I love the metallic flecks in the deep-blue paint and how they sparkle in the sun. Actually, I really love this car. I don't know if I can get rid of it.*

Ouch! I have never given this subject much thought, but I am being strongly pressed to take inventory of my life, to measure the worth of my goals, ambitions, dreams, and possessions against the worth of living a life totally surrendered to God.

"I . . . I'm not sure I would have asked for help if I had known this was coming," I whisper out loud, realizing I am wrestling with my Lord. "I've never given idols much thought." They were obvious throughout the Old Testament, but seriously? Nowadays? Idols?

I can't escape.

Lord, we're instructed to love You with our whole heart, soul, mind, and strength. So, I suppose an idol is anything or anyone that gets most of our heart, soul, mind, and strength. To whom or what do we turn for strength or security or hope? From whom do we get strength besides You?

What *is* taking my time, strength, money, passion? Sports. Jobs. Possessions. Relationships. Reputation. Education. The stark truth is that idols litter my life, and the time has come to deal with my choices, my loves, and my most glaring idol, my car. I look to the heavens and exhale a sigh of surrender. No more idols. No more. It is as if I have been given new eyes, and now I want a new heart to match the truth that has just been revealed.

Release who and what means the most to me . . .

I envision Abraham tying Isaac to the altar and raising his knife to kill him. The son of promise. The son miraculously given to Abraham and Sarah in their old age. Abraham releasing him, giving him up as an offering. Abraham's total obedience. God's amazing response—"Don't touch him. Now I know that you fear God since you've not withheld your only son from Me."

Clarity crashes over me like a breaking wave as I stand there. For the first time, I see the passionate love and the ultimate trust that bound Abraham and God together. That made them one. That made Abraham's obedience to a wild, costly command automatic. That made God's heart spill over with love for him and for his single-minded devotion to God.

I want that. I ache for that same kind of relationship. I hunger to know God's heart so well that obedience, any obedience, will be quick and complete. I want Him to trust me with any outlandish request, any unreasonable command. I want Him to be sure that I would obey, that I will understand His heart, His passion behind the command. I want Him alone to be my strength and support and help. I want no other gods.

"Yes, my Lord. I *want* only You," I declare aloud.

"Uh, excuse me. Is that your car?"

Jerked suddenly to attention, I turn toward the voice and blurt, "Huh?"

"Miss? Miss? Sorry to startle you, but is that your car?" asked a young man who seemed to have come out of nowhere.

"Uh, yeah, that's my, a, tha – that's my car," I stutter.

"Would you ever consider selling it? A 350 Malibu convertible is almost impossible to find. It's worth a lot, you know."

"Uh . . . yeah. They . . . uh . . . are . . . are hard to find. I've . . . uh . . . had this one a long time."

"Well, here's my card. *Please* call me. I want this car and am willing to pay what it is worth," he presses.

"Oh. Um . . . yeah. I will call you," I stammer back.

"No. I mean it. I will pay top dollar. Please call me," he pushes.

"Okay," I say, taking his card while sliding into the familiar cream-colored seat. I hit the ignition, the headers purring nicely, drowning out his final plea. I wave good-bye to his last, "Please . . . call meeeeee!"

Usually, I drive right on the top edge of the speed limit and choose the highways, but not today. I choose the back roads, the quiet, less-traveled roads, keeping the "purring" soft so I can think.

I had argued with God. I had asked Him for help, and He had responded. I hadn't liked His answer, so I had wrestled with Him. I hadn't liked Roy's "Just have some faith," either. What if faith brings a distasteful answer? What if He meets the need in a way that bends or breaks or even shatters my wants? What if I don't want to listen? To obey? To accept His choice? What if He puts His finger on an idol? What if I must repent of looking to other gods for strength or help or guidance or provision? Or simply loving things?

86

I can't ignore the facts this time any more than I could when I first met Roy. I analyze God's intervention, all of it. A job *had* appeared out of nowhere—a job that matched my passion; a job that connected me and my car with a buyer in that town, at that school, at just the right time, practically begging me to sell him the car; a job that led me to God's miraculous provision.

Now, the question isn't, "Could I?" or "Would I?" What had been only hypothetical questions an hour ago have now become the very direct and personal questions: "*Will* you? *Will* you give up something that means a lot to you for My sake? For My service? *Will* you let go of something that you've held tightly— that has been the fulfillment of a dream? That has taken so much of your time, money, energy, and love?"

My 350 certainly doesn't compare to Abraham's Isaac, but the message is the same. I call the man as soon as I get home. His check covers the total cost of the two-week mission trip to Eastern Europe.

I gave up my idol, and God gave me the world.

That's who God is.

That's what God does.

"IDOLS" – FOR DEEPER THOUGHT . . .

1. Deuteronomy 6:5 says, "You shall love the Lord your God with all your heart and with all your soul and with all your might." As you think about your relationship with God, where do you lack full commitment? What changes would you like to make?

2. In Matthew 10:39 (NIV), Jesus says this: "Whoever finds his life will lose it, and whoever loses his life for my sake will find it." How does this truth encourage you to release whatever may be becoming an idol in your life?

3. Moses burns the golden calf idol to powder and chastises the Israelites for looking to an idol for guidance. He gives them a choice to turn back to the LORD or suffer the great consequences. What do you do when you need guidance? To whom or what do you go? Why?

4. When you are fearful or in need of direction, why would seeking the LORD be the wisest choice? What difference would it make in your life?

5. Moses prays, "Alas, this people has committed a great sin, and they have made a god of gold for themselves. But now, if You will, forgive their sin (Exodus 32:31–32). What conversation do you need to have with the Lord as you think about your life?

6. In this day and age, our idol probably isn't a golden calf, but the bottom line is the same. What gets the most of our time, attention, love, effort, money, thoughts? Is it education, money, success, control, food, drink, sex, relationships, entertainment, children, goals? Talk with the Lord about what idolatry looks like in your own life. What change do you need to make to turn to the Lord with your whole heart, soul, mind, and strength?

Idols

All things that were gain to me, now
I count but loss.
My Lord, have Your way with me, and
take me to Your cross.
I want to know You.
(Philippians 3:7–14)

Unusable but Used

The few weeks prior to the mission trip were filled with preparation meetings and prayer times. Several of us began to congeal into a cohesive unit, and they drew me in as if I was not a total stranger. I shared a little here and there, but as for the deep hurts and brokenness that were choking me, I resolutely remained silent.

This team-building process coaxed all of us to a depth of transparency that I both feared and craved. Ambivalence tossed me back and forth like a tiny boat in stormy seas. My fear kept pressing me to ask Roy to remove my name from the list, but then the assurance of that first moment, now strengthened by many moments with these dear brothers and sisters in Christ, restrained me. Yet I felt caught. I knew I was supposed to go on this trip, but I also knew I was not being authentic with the team members. Worse yet, I *couldn't* be real with them. I couldn't tell them I was recovering from another freefall into the lesbian lifestyle. That I was raw. That I was afraid and fragile.

In addition, the Lord's words from Revelation 2:4 were piercing my heart. "You have left your first love." While the team prepared their hearts for service, I was forced to face the truth of the condition of mine: I had left my walk with Jesus, even though He had saved me from a suicide attempt years before.

But the team meetings had ignited an increasing hunger for godly relationships, and I sensed that the fulfillment was within reach. It was close. Too near to stop, but also too scary to become vulnerable to the group and risk the truth surfacing. I was both desperate to run away and desperate to continue.

With this internal battle still raging, I boarded the plane. I firmly tucked my turmoil out of sight and wondered at the strange "knowing" that compelled me forward. I wondered about the others. Did they "know" too? Were their realities playing sneaky games with them? Were they frightened at all about what they might find in new countries or, worse yet, in themselves? One by one, overhead lights clicked off, and soft sleep sounds filled the air. I closed my eyes and heard His love whispering hope, bringing soft light to my darkness. A new path—so sweet but steep, steeper than I was strong—stretched before me. I headed into the absolute unknown, toward Vienna and Eastern Europe so recently freed from Communism's grip. The similarities to my own circumstances moved me, and something inside awakened. It was hope—for myself and them.

In the darkness of the plane, I heard team members softly chattering about being used by God. I remained silent, feeling totally unusable and deeply vulnerable. They expected miracles. I just hoped for a strand of strength to walk the steep path toward wholeness again.

Seventeen hours later, we landed, and our host families hustled us to their homes. We grabbed a little real sleep in real beds, and at 6:00 a.m. thcir time, 10:00 p.m. on our own clocks—we headed to the convention center for our first meeting.

In their first gulp of freedom, thousands of people from a dozen countries poured into the Vienna Convention Center, finally free to worship and travel and reach for dreams. The atmosphere was electric. At least a dozen different languages swirled around me, filling the arena with expectancy. Goose bumps covered me. God was there, and He wanted to touch these dear people as much as they wanted to touch Him.

We were pulled into a current of powerful faith and transparent expectation. Though our bodies begged for more sleep, the love and passion and hunger for God of these people sped us forward into their time zone, into decades of buried hopes suddenly unearthed by freedom.

How I was to fit in was still quite a mystery. I just wanted to be where He was. My own heart began to beat with modest expectancy. Somehow, I resonated with the throngs. It was like we embraced a common opportunity to move from captivity to freedom.

The team strategically disbursed throughout the auditorium, our bright-yellow "ministry team" name tags clearly visible, as the first song began. In a déjà-vu moment, Roy waved his hands and stopped the musicians.

Does he always do this? I wondered.

He then took the microphone and shot an arrow of absolute terror through me.

"I believe God is here to heal backs. If you have a back problem, find someone with a yellow ministry team name tag, and he or she will pray for you."

My thoughts raced. A gripping fear tightened my chest and panic stole my breath. Based on my past, I probably needed ministering to more than anyone here, and at that moment, I was an emotional mess! Furthermore, I hated the popular "name it and claim it" gospel stuff and wasn't at all sure God was going to heal backs. *I have to escape,* I told myself. *I can't help anyone!* Thank God that Roy's proclamation in English required three translations. It gave me time to peel my yellow tag off and hustle to the nearest exit.

Six stairs from the door, my worst nightmare happened. A wizened, humpbacked woman stepped into the aisle and grabbed my arm. A landslide of tears and words tumbled out, and her desperation overpowered mine. A strong presence enveloped both of us. I pressed my crumpled nametag back on and slipped her trembling, arthritic hands into mine. I mean, what choice did I have?

Quite supernaturally, our hearts touched. No "language" barrier there. Our common anguish intertwined us like tightly woven wicker. Tears streamed from her timid blue eyes that looked like pools of pain.

Oh, God. I have no clue what to do. You know how I feel about all this healing stuff, and you know how I feel about myself. Please, Lord, help me help this dear woman. Have Your way, Lord, I prayed silently.

I pointed to my wrinkled name tag. "Kathy. My name is Kathy."

She tapped her chest. "Zdena."

Just then Roy's wife, Mary, and an interpreter, Hilga, joined us. I glanced at Mary, expecting her to take over. After all, she was a pastor's wife, and her husband got us into this in the first place. She, however, gave me a slight shrug and made it quite clear that I was to take the lead.

Yeah, right. If you only knew. I'm not even fit to be here, let alone take the lead.

Turning to Zdena and shaking hands, I whispered the only words that came to mind: "Let's pray." Hilga translated it, and the four of us turned to the Lord, waiting to hear His words and His will for this moment in time. Silently I asked for His heart for this crooked, bent woman. I asked Him to do what only He can do. "Your Kingdom come, Lord, to this woman. Your will be done." I felt moved to lay my hands on her back. Shocked, my eyes shot open. Not only did her back curve like a capital S, it was also bent at the shoulders like a tight question mark! Mary, Hilga, and Zdena still had their eyes closed, listening, waiting, but I couldn't go on. My faith was fragile, my own heartache just one heartbeat from spilling over, and I got this back! The panic that had pushed me toward the exit moments before stormed back. *I have nothing to give this poor crippled woman!* The thought paralyzed me.

Instantaneously, a feathery wisp of air touched me, and I sensed the Lord's presence and His smile. "It's easier to surrender and let Me work when one is empty and helpless and simply available," He whispered into my spirit.

Well, I am available, Lord. Thank You.

A sweet calmness covered me, replacing my crippling misgivings, and I began: "Lord, please give Zdena what she needs. Open a door, Lord, for her." Hilga, our interpreter, translated this, and instantly her weeping stopped. She lifted her head as far as her humped back allowed and quickly turned to Hilga. Words poured from Zdena like an urgent waterfall over sharp rocks. Mary and I leaned in and struggled to make sense of German and Hungarian and, as Hilga could squeeze it in, some sporadic English. The Lord had surely moved, and Zdena had passionately responded.

Several minutes passed. Then Hilga made a stop sign with her hands, took a few deep breaths, and gave Mary and me a very condensed summary.

"Zdena has carried a weight for years. It's a blackness that seeks to devour her, little by little. She feels powerless against its might. It has stolen her health and often her will to live."

Stunned, memories of my suicide attempt and my latest sinful fall flashed in my mind. What on earth was I thinking to even come on this trip!

Mary gave another shrug; Hilga waited to interpret what came next, and Zdena looked at me—looked through me. I knew this kind of pain.

I said aloud this time, "Well, let's pray. Lord, please give this woman what she needs." This woman? Something shifted inside me, but I couldn't quite grasp it. A somber pause followed as we waited upon the Lord.

"Kathy, ask Zdena if she has a crooked relationship." My eyes popped open again, and my head jerked up, startling all three women.

LORD! Really? I silently blurted to Him.

"Did you get something?" Mary asked. "What did you hear?"

Zdena didn't speak, but our eyes locked.

"Well . . ." *Lord. I can't ask her that. Well, can I? Who am I to talk about someone else's bad relationships?* My prayer suddenly echoed in my spirit: *"Give this woman what she needs." Oh Lord, I get it.* He will give both of us what we need. *What an amazing Lord You are,* I whispered only to Him.

Humbly but expectantly, I slipped the little woman's gnarled hands into mine and asked, "Zdena, do you have a crooked relationship?"

Hilga moved my question through her German so that Zdena could change it into her Hungarian. In breathless spurts, she recounted the day, almost fifty years prior, when she kicked her son out of her home and her life.

We nodded and tenderly placed our hands on Zdena's back again. After all, if Roy was right, God wanted to heal her back as well as her heart.

Forgiveness is all I heard. I glanced at Mary and Hilga, but they were silent. Perhaps from my own brokenness, I asked two questions this time.

"Zdena, can you forgive your son? Can you forgive yourself?" She nodded after Hilga translated, and more Hungarian poured out. Hilga summed up the response. "Forgive my son? Easily. But forgive myself? That's another story."

She shared unabashedly, completely. My heart broke for her as she battled to forgive herself. It seemed guilt was always the last to leave, but it too finally burst forth like wild waters suddenly loosed as the Lord Himself demolished the dam that had confined it for decades.

Snap! Snap! Crack! Snap! The exact sounds of a chiropractic adjustment rang out right from under our very own hands, Zdena's back straightened! Vertebrae moved! They literally moved! Realigned! God straightened her crooked spine right smack under our very own hands! We heard it! We felt it! We watched it! Within minutes, Zdena's head no longer hung. She was four to five inches taller and looked straight at us, her eyes wide and wild with amazement.

I could barely take it all in. My own crooked life had somehow straightened, too. The Almighty God breathed life into us; the damage and debris from our crooked relationship was healed by forgiveness. Brokenness was turned to wholeness by the nail-scarred hands of Jesus.

We couldn't contain ourselves. We praised and cried and hugged and praised some more, slowly becoming aware that similar things were happening throughout the building.

Divine encounters with God. Chains of bondage broken. Years of oppression lifted. Humble, hungry people meeting with the God of grace.

Zdena and I were permanently interwoven in the tapestry of the forgiven.

God's boundless mercy healed two crooked women that day.

The King of Kings used the unusable.

"UNUSABLE BUT USED" –
FOR DEEPER THOUGHT . . .

1. What hidden things do you feel shameful about?

2. In 1 John 1:7 (NIV) God says, "But if we walk in the light, as He is in the light, we have fellowship with one another, and the blood of Jesus, His Son, purifies us from all sin." What would change in your life if you would bring those hidden things into the light?

3. What friendships or blessings have you missed out on because shame silenced you?

4. In Ephesians 5:11 (NIV) God says, "Have nothing to do with the fruitless deeds of darkness, but rather expose them." How could God use what you may have hidden to minister to someone else if you were brave enough to be transparent?

5. How important is it for you to guard your reputation, and what has it cost you?

6. In Matthew 10:27 Jesus says, "What I tell you in the darkness, speak in the light; and what you hear whispered in your ear, proclaim upon the housetops." Is there something you learned during a dark time in your life that the Lord could use to benefit someone else?

7. "If we confess our sins, He is faithful and just and will forgive us our sins and purify us from all unrighteousness" (1 John 1:9 NIV). Whom do you need to forgive and how can you begin that process? Do you need to forgive yourself and move on from guilt and shame? Set aside time to do just that and record your findings.

Unusable but Used

Oh the eyes of the Lord are searchin' to
and fro over all the earth.
They are lookin' for a person
surrendered in heart.
They are lookin' for a person who is
dead to self walkin' in humility
(2 Chronicles 16:9)

Do the Works

I scooted into the restroom to lose her. I darted behind the nearest open door and snapped the latch shut. Holding my breath, I listened, fiercely attentive. My eyes were riveted on the opening at the bottom of the door. The heavy footsteps of solid boots rang out. Metal taps clicked on the cold stone floor. *Click. Click.* The sound stopped at my door. Silver pentagrams imbedded in black leather glowed white hot. Or so it seemed. I squeezed my eyes shut and pressed sweaty palms over them. *Oh God! What now?* I thought.

The entire auditorium in Vienna had continued to throb with expectation as the four thousand Christians had kept coming each night to meet with their God—openly. No secret police dragging them to jail. No spies. No fear. Each night the same build-up: Musicians tuning guitars. Speakers testing microphones. Team members directing scores of interpreters. The entire facility buzzing! Bursting to praise God for freedom.

Upon arriving the second day, I had scampered up the stairs to the upper balcony, content to just blend in, but after my experience with God's healing of Zdena's back, I was thrilled to be there and to watch God meet the needs of these precious believers. I had claimed the aisle seat in the first row so that I could welcome these saints as they passed by to find their own seats. I longed to speak their languages and know their stories. I ached to have their faith, the faith that had sustained them through so much abuse and hate and suffering.

A new friend and fellow team member, Kevin, slipped into the seat next to me, and a strange relief covered me. Minutes before Pastor Roy took the microphone, four young people, maybe college aged, headed up the stairs. Kevin and I had seen them the night before, all dressed in black with chains and pentagrams hanging from ears and noses and necks and clothes and belts. We nodded and smiled. They shot back icy glances.

As they climbed up the stairs behind us, a disturbing darkness invaded that pocket of the arena. We turned and watched them take the highest seats . . . the ones tucked just under the steel ceiling beams . . . the ones in the dimmest light.

"Oh my," Kevin whispered. I nodded and let out a long, measured breath. They picked *our* section. Again. We didn't say it out loud, but we both felt it. Not exactly a dread but a sobering, a feeling that God had brought them to our section on purpose and that He had something for them. I mean, we had "ministry team" stickers on, and these kids sure needed ministry.

We had seen them on the first day. Then on Tuesday, we had determined that things would be different. We actually blocked their path up to the top seats, shook their hands, and told them our names. No response, but the ice in their eyes wasn't quite as sharp as they headed up to their dark seats.

By Thursday, they actually gave us their names before heading to their seats. I repeated them over and over to myself so I wouldn't forget: Sonja, Bjorn, Yurka, and Olga.

Friday, however, things took a wild turn. Sonja, the scariest of the four, started stalking me. Every step I took, she followed— even to the bathroom. Right there, in her black pointed boots with silver imbedded pentagrams, she was waiting for me. *Okay, Lord. Help me, please.* I unlatched the door, and evil met me. Pure evil. "Comme on! Come onnn, Christian. Cast me out. Come on!" she growled. People raced out of the bathroom, leaving me alone with Sonja. I was no match for this evil that sought to swallow me, but I knew the power of Jesus's name. I inhaled, straightened, and searched her face for the person Jesus died for.

"Sonja, Jesus lov—"

She screamed and twisted as if I had knifed her. I turned and fled the bathroom while she writhed, but I knew she wouldn't be far behind.

It began again, softly, quietly. "Comme on. Come on, Christian. Cast me ooout," came the mocking grating voice— not human. I knew that. I hustled into the arena to find Pastor Mark. After all, he was a well-known pastor, and if anyone could cast out a demon, he could. My pace increased. Sonja's did too. Louder now. "Comme onn, Christian! Afrrraid? Hahhh ha ha." The maniacal, guttural voice shot shivers through me.

Almost running, I spotted him. "Pastor Mark! Pastor Mark! I need your help!" He moved toward me but looked beyond me at Sonja, who was running right behind me and closing in.

"She wants the demon cast out of her," I blurted. "I told her you were the man to do it."

"No worries," he quipped and moved into Sonja's path. He said a five-second prayer and turned to go, leaving her untouched and with a malevolent spirit deriding his ineptness.

109

I ran to my seat and gave Kevin a quick heads up. We knew God was doing something but had no clue how to join Him in it.

That night, as the ministry team debriefed, we learned that similar encounters were happening throughout the auditorium. Almost every team member had some kind of demonic encounter.

Agitation filled my sleep that night. I finally slipped to my knees and asked the Lord about it. He instantly rebuked me. "If I choose to free a captive through you, you say, 'Yes, Lord.' You don't take them to someone I'm not using."

"Yes, Lord. I'm sorry. Please give me another chance to be You to Sonja," I whispered, half afraid that He would do just that, and I crawled back into bed.

Earlier than usual Saturday morning, we piled into vans, knowing we needed extra time to pray throughout the arena. We sensed the Lord would move in the miraculous, and we were desperate for some quiet time to get in tune with His plan for the day. While the team finished praying and worshiping the Lord told me to go lay on the seats of those four young people. *Lord, that's kinda weird,* I thought. Instantly He reminded me of Elijah laying on the widow's dead son and bringing him back to life. I slipped into the cavernous auditorium and hustled up to where these lost kids always sat. I flipped down all four seats, stretched myself over them, and prayed for light and life . . . light and life . . . light and life . . . for God-breathed life.

Some time later, people began pouring into the arena, and I found our seats. Immediately, I heard the Lord say, "Too much in the light." This time, I responded right out loud, "That's kinda weird, Lord." But I moved up several rows, into dimmer lighting. Kevin joined me, and we waited to greet our "fab four," as we now called them.

"I think we're growing on 'em," Kevin joked. Nervous little laughs followed. I mean, really. Being reminded of what Elijah did, we had an idea that God may use us to do a similar kind of thing, and that realization brought a unique uneasiness and an equally unique expectancy.

Sure, we've all read that Jesus told His disciples they would do the works He did and even greater works, but here we were, sitting with four demon-possessed youngsters, the "work's to do" waiting for us! Unique uneasiness and expectancy is an understatement.

Our four "friends" headed our way, breaking into my wild thoughts. We boldly blocked their path, shook their hands, offered them the seats next to us, and they took them! *Yikes! Now what?* We hadn't really expected this. I shot a glance up at their usual seats. They were bathed in bright light. No wonder they didn't head up there. I elbowed Kevin to take a look. Filled with awe, we glanced toward heaven and smiled. God doing what only He can do.

At various times we grabbed small conversations with all four, and we managed to move, somewhat awkwardly, through the day. East Germans, hooked on drugs, cult members, cutters, sacrificers—the list went on and on. The darkness was thick, but always God was right in the midst where two or three were gathered.

Sonja still stalked me but no longer mocked me. The power that held her had weakened while the reality that Jesus was working all over the arena was strengthening me. I knew Jesus was ever-so-lovingly inching me into my second chance.

The evening worship began, and all four bolted. They flew out the nearest doors, unable to endure the Lord who inhabits the praises of His people. Kevin and I both let out small sighs of relief but immediately prayed that the Lord would force them to come back on Sunday.

We debriefed that evening and lingered long in prayer, simple prayer—"Your Kingdom come tomorrow. Your will be done," knowing full well that scores of captives would be freed.

Kevin and I spent our Sunday pre-worship prayer time in our six seats. We begged the Lord to bring our four friends back. To free them. To fill them with light and life.

The arena sprang to life as thousands filled the seats and aisles and every empty area. Electric expectancy! The worship team tuned and tested mics. Pastor Roy paced and prayed, getting ready to speak. Just as the lead singer began to pray, our four friends showed up to join us. What a rush! God was ready. His servants were ready. Satan was on edge.

Worship began, and the Spirit flooded the arena. Demons screamed, and every demonic encounter in the New Testament raced through my mind.

I turned to Sonja. She screeched and fled. Meanwhile, Bjorn brushed up my back as he levitated out of his seat. I turned to him. He crashed back down, foaming at the mouth, banging his head on his seat. Kevin had Yurka. Olga took Sonja's place behind me, her hot breath on my neck. I touched Bjorn and said, "Jesus, come!" He flew out of his seat again, suspended in thin air, writhing, still foaming. "Jesus, come!" Bam! He crashed back down, smacking his head on his chair. I threw my arms around his head. "Come out!" He melted—still and silent.

Oh, Lord! He's dead! I thought. *Come, Lord Jesus. Come! Jesus! Come!*

He stiffened, sat straight up, and growled. His brown eyes turned blood red. He cursed and hissed at me. Shaken, the only thing I could think of to say was, "Jesus. Jesus. Jesus." A violent seizure shook him like a rag doll, taking him out of his seat and then slamming him back down, unconscious again.

Olga leaned on my back. In a raspy voice dripping with venom, she snarled, "Do yooouu want to knooow our name?"

I turned and said, "No!"

Her blue eyes turned cat-like yellow with thin slivers of black running top to bottom. Through grinding teeth she growled, "We arrrre Pilatus. We killllled the Christ."

"Shut up!" I ordered. She instantly ran, screeching and hissing, white foam spraying from her mouth as she ran.

I turned to Bjorn and began again. "More, Lord Jesus. More." The violence of each spasm lessened as the demons left, one by one—seven of them in all. "Bjorn," I whispered as I wrapped my arms around his shoulders and searched his soft-brown eyes for life. "Bjorn, Jesus loves you. Jesus loves you," I said over and over until he came to. "Bjorn, ask Jesus to come into your life. Ask Him now to take control of your life."

I waited and prayed and listened to the Spirit setting people free throughout the entire arena. Sounds of hell's presence were diminishing, screams and screeches turning to sobs and prayers and songs. Little pockets of life and worship springing up everywhere. The sweetness of Jesus filled dark pits with His presence, His light and love.

Bjorn finally, softly, began talking with Jesus. My tears mixed with his as He asked Jesus to save him, to take control, to change him, to heal him.

Eventually, a deep stillness bathed the arena. The Spirit walked among us, tending the sheep—healing hearts, filling voids, bringing truth. The quiet hum of intimate conversations followed. I visited with Bjorn about finding a Bible-teaching church, about leaving present friends and finding new ones, about reading the Word and walking in the Spirit. I read Scriptures to him. We prayed.

God was working in small groups all over the arena, setting captives free.

Sonja and Olga eventually rejoined us, light and life sparkling in their eyes. The six of us held hands and poured out our hearts to the Lord. I shared my failures with them and how it was God's amazing grace that I was even in Vienna. The kids shared tragic stories. We all shed tears and praised our Lord.

Long past lunchtime, Roy quietly announced that we'd resume the conference in an hour. Our four friends left, but Kevin and I sat and shared. He told me he saw other team members intercept both Sonja and Olga, and he told me about his time with Yurka. He left to grab a sandwich. I stayed, sobered and silent in God's awesome presence, absolutely humbled by my second chance.

When we reconvened, I moved down to the first row, the seat I had chosen the very first day. Kevin and the fab four joined me just before worship started, all four now dressed in new clothes of various lively colors. Everything about them spoke of new life.

A young man from the worship team took the microphone for just a few minutes to explain what the Spirit had just done and to reiterate the crucial steps to ensure growth in Christ. Then he turned our hearts toward the throne.

How can I explain the worship of that evening? The worship of our four friends—hands raised, tears overflowing from new, circumcised hearts? The worship of people who'd been crushed for decades but who were mounting up with wings like eagles before our very eyes? The worship of those the Lord had decided to use to do His works?

Pastor Roy never did speak that Sunday. Jesus did. His kingdom came. His will was done. He cast out hoards of demons and fed His precious lambs Himself, the living Bread. This fear-ridden, oppressed multitude was freed by the love of the Lord Himself. This motley ministry team from the United States became His hands, His feet, His voice.

Staggering.

I came clothed in regret and shame, just hoping that my first love, Jesus, might touch and restore me, yet again. To Him who does abundantly, exceedingly beyond all that we ask or think, to Him be all glory and praise!

"DO THE WORKS" – FOR DEEPER THOUGHT . . .

1. Have you ever given much thought to the spiritual battle going on all around us? We can't fight if we don't know there is a fight. The crucial truth in the battle is to know that God's power is almighty. Satan's power is extremely limited. What steps are you moved to take to be better informed?

2. Matthew 8:16 gives us a glimpse into part of Jesus's ministry. "When evening came, they brought to Him many who were demon-possessed; and He cast out the spirits with a word, and healed all who were ill." The gospels record several instances of Jesus healing other demon-possessed people. While we are not to look for such encounters, we may find ourselves in a situation where the Lord may use us in such a way. How can you be ready?

3. In 1 John 4 we're told about spirits that confess Jesus as Lord and spirits that don't. Then John declares in verse 4: "You are from God, little children, and have overcome them; because greater is He who is in you than he who is in the world." How does this encourage you to have no fear and to be ready if God should choose to use you in this spiritual battle?

4. Peter also gives powerful counsel in 1 Peter 5:8–9: "Be of sober spirit, be on the alert. Your adversary, the devil, prowls around like a roaring lion, seeking someone to devour. But resist him, firm in your faith, knowing that the same experiences of suffering are being accomplished by your brethren who are in the world." How does this strengthen you?

5. In James 4:7 we read, "Submit therefore to God. Resist the devil and he will flee from you." What do you learn here about your role and the devil's limited power?

6. Paul gives amazing counsel in Ephesians 6:10–17 about resisting evil.

"Finally, be strong in the Lord and in the strength of His might. Put on the full armor of God, so that you will be able to stand firm against the schemes of the devil. For our struggle is not against flesh and blood, but against the rulers, against the powers, against the world forces of this darkness, against the spiritual forces of wickedness in the heavenly places. Therefore, take up the full armor of God, so that you will be able to resist in the evil day, and having done everything, to stand firm. Stand firm therefore, having girded your loins with truth, and having put on the breastplate of righteousness, and having shod your feet with the preparation of the gospel of peace; in addition to all, taking up the shield of faith with which you will be able to extinguish all the flaming arrows of the evil one. And take the helmet of salvation, and the sword of the Spirit, which is the word of God."

Record your thoughts and questions as you soak in these verses.

Do The Works

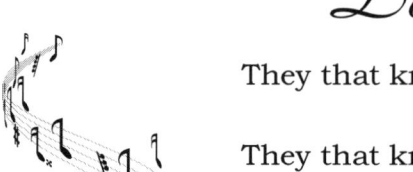

They that know their God shall be strong
and do valiantly.
They that know their God shall be strong
and do mighty deeds.
He is their strength. He is their sword.
He is their God. He is their Lord.
(Daniel 11:32)

Available

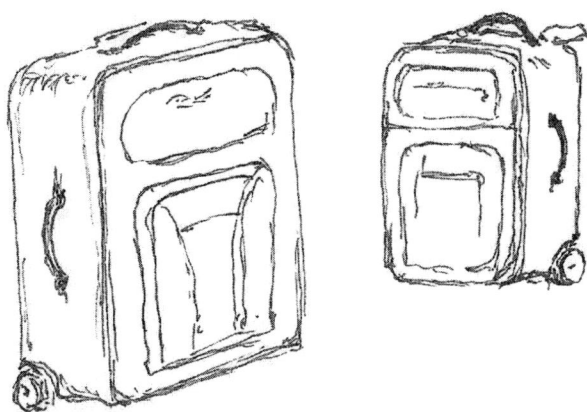

After our wild week in Vienna, we broke into ten teams of seven with each team heading to specific countries for the second week of this mission trip. I spent that week in what was then Czechoslovakia, fell in love with the people, and somehow felt that I'd be back.

I returned to the US with Isaiah's words burning in my heart, "Here am I, Lord; send me." A dear friend had attended Youth With a Mission schools, and I longed to jump into a YWam Discipleship Training School (DTS) being offered locally. There, I would wait for God's call to return to Czechoslovakia.

I zipped through the last two weeks at YWAM and fixed my eyes on the Czech Republic, elated that the Lord was sending me back. The intrigue of how He would work out all the details began in earnest.

"Hey, Pat! What's up?" My cousin, who only calls once or twice a year, phoned to ask me to stop by on my way to the travel agent. Yep. A travel agent. I mean, this *was* 1989. So I did.

"Well, the Lord told me to give you this," she answered and handed me a small sealed envelope folded in half, which I absentmindedly stuffed into my pocket. "So, what's going on with you?"

I spilled the news that I was heading overseas. We shouted mutual praises to the Lord, and I scooted off to the travel agency.

After some research, the agent said, "Well, the cheapest ticket into Prague is around $1,200."

"$1,200? There must be another way!" I wailed.

She shuffled through some more papers and came up with an alternative. "All right, if you're willing to fly into Frankfurt, then take the train to Vienna, then take another train north to Brno, and if you are willing to buy a one-way ticket, we can do it for $410."

"Let's do it!" I exclaimed. "Ten dollars is all I have right now, but I'll give you the rest when the Lord provides it."

Her face wrinkled up like a raisin. "What?"

I dug $10 out of my pocket, the folded envelope coming with it. Curious, I opened it and was dumbfounded by what I found inside—a check for $400!

"Yeah, God. He just provided!" Poor lady. She almost quit breathing. I signed the check, handed her the full amount, and accepted the ticket in return. What a great confirmation from the Lord! He provided right up front because *He* was sending me. I was His, and this trip was His. I packed, enjoyed a great send-off party, and waited for my departure day to finally arrive.

Marveling at how the Lord worked out the ticket money, I settle back in my seat on the plane and try to imagine what teaching in the Czech Republic will be like. I know nothing about teaching English as a second language, but I do know that the Lord equips His children for what He calls them to do. *He won't fail me,* I tell myself.

About three hours into the flight, however, my peace flips to pure panic. *What on earth am I doing? I've never been overseas by myself. I'm such a homebody. I don't know another language. I'm flying into Frankfurt, Germany. On a one-way ticket. Yikes and more yikes!*

My thoughts race. *Honestly, Kathy. Why are you doing this? What were you thinking?* My breathing quickens, and my imagination kicks into overdrive. Thoughts of Frankfurt, the biggest travel hub in Europe, crash over me like giant waves. Just before I hyperventilate and pass out, a kind flight attendant lays her hand on my shoulder and asks if I need something.

"Uh, yes. Um, I need off, yeah, I need off this plane," I stammer.

Stunned, she stoops and places a hand on my forehead. "Are you having a medical emergency? Does the pilot need to land at the nearest terminal?"

"Well, no, not exactly. I just, um, I guess, well, I'll be okay. Really. I'm okay."

"We will have a lengthy layover in Boston," she explains, worry lines still furrowing her brow. "We can get you help there."

"Oh, good. Thanks," I assure her.

As we approach Logan International in Boston, the pilot announces that the plane to Frankfurt is overbooked. He asks if there are any passengers who would be willing to stay in

Boston and goes on to explain that they would be refunded the price of their ticket.

Great! I'll stay, visit my sister, get my money back, and then head back to Colorado! Relief washes over me with this new plan in hand and the terrible notions of Frankfurt out of the picture. I join the competitive scramble to get my name on the refund list, find out that I am number twelve on that list, find the nearest seat, dig into my snack bag, and take out a book.

Immediately, the Lord breaks into my thoughts. *Kathy, you said, "Here am I, Lord; send me." And I did provide your ticket, didn't I?*

I can't ignore His questioning as I think about that $400 check. *Oh, Lord, I'm sorry. Yes, I did ask You to send me, and You did get me that ticket. Lord, please don't let them call my name. I'm afraid, but it would break my heart to disobey and disappoint You. I do want to be sent by You,* I reply silently, repentantly, and repeatedly, trying hard to convince myself. My uneasiness ebbs and flows as I try harder to concentrate on my book.

Eventually, the loudspeaker comes to life. "Attention passengers. Will numbers one through eleven report to the desk for your refund? All other passengers heading to Frankfurt proceed to Gate 204. Boarding will begin in five minutes."

Oh, thank You, Lord!

Relief mixes with fragile confidence as I head to gate 204, knowing nothing but the One who is sending me.

Several hours pass, and I suddenly realize I am flying over the ocean. Fear attacks again. *Oh, Lord! Please come and sit next to me.* I place my hand on the empty seat next to me, hoping He will show up somehow, some way. I close my eyes and force my thoughts toward faith. I think back to all the biographies I have read about missionaries and how the Lord showed up for them and how He sent angels to render service to them.

At just that second, four words resound in my spirit. *I walk with angels.* It is not as if I am saying it to myself. It isn't even as if the Lord is saying it to me. It just is. It is a *knowing*, and it completely overtakes me. Fear flees. Confidence soars.
Great expectancy rises within me, and a verse from Hebrews comes to mind: "[Angels are] ministering spirits, sent out to render service for the sake of those who will inherit salvation" (Hebrews 1:14).

As I think of the many angelic visitors throughout Scripture, a verse from Psalms arises in my spirit: "For He shall give His angels charge over you, to keep you in all your ways" (Psalm 91:11 KJV).

"That's it, isn't it, Lord? I walk with angels! You provided the ticket and now You are providing the protection! Thank You, Lord," I whisper aloud and pat the seat next to me, knowing He has indeed shown up. I settle back and drift into a sleep of deep contentment, safe in His provision of those He would send to help me.

Hours later, the pilot's voice breaks the silence. "We are approaching Frankfurt. Fasten your seat belts and prepare for landing."

Fear flares up, but the declaration *I walk with angels* echoes within and quenches it. Excitement begins to bubble up as I wonder just what Frankfurt will be like. I had been to Europe once but never Germany. I know no other language, and I know zero about what to do once we land. *Those angels better be on their toes, Lord,* I chuckle to myself.

Frankfurt Airport *and* Train Station. Sheer pandemonium! Thousands of people going in a dozen directions to and from trains and trams, planes and buses. Multiple languages blend into a wild cacophony where nothing is understandable.

I know that I need to get a train to Vienna, so I approach what looks like a ticket window. Patience is running very thin throughout the mob, and several people shout various things at me. Sensing their annoyance, I am thankful that I *don't* know any other language.

Finally, after the fifth window, I get a ticket and, piecing together crazy instructions and wild gestures, I get the general drift that the train station is underneath the airport, and that I need to hurry, as my train is approaching.

In addition to my carry-on bag, I have two suitcases, one of which is full of books. Thinking that wasn't sufficient, I had also packed more books among my clothes in the other suitcase. I soon discover my huge mistake.

Trying to hurry, I swing my heavy carry-on, which also contains books, over my shoulder and try to ease my luggage carrier onto the escalator. The weight, however, smashes the two small wheels the minute it hits the first step. The luggage heaves forward. The bungee cords snaps. Both suitcases hurtle down the steps. The first breaks open as it hits the floor, flinging books everywhere. The second breaks open, spewing clothing and *more* books everywhere. And my train is pulling in.

Lord! I walk with angels, and I sure need one right now to render service!

I begin to frantically gather books when I hear, "Howdy, ma'am. It seems you need some help," in perfect southern English. An American sailor immediately goes to work. In no time, books are repacked and clothes are stuffed in. He looks at my ticket and urgently nudges me toward the train that is just then inching out of the station. "Hurry, ma'am! You jump on. I'll throw your bags in," he yells above the noise of trains coming and going. I jog and jump aboard. He runs beside the train with both bags, throwing one in while on a trot and the other on a dead run. He smiles and waves good-bye. Hoisting my last bag up the steps, I turn to yell thanks, but I don't see a sailor anywhere.

Oh, God! Thank You.

I lug the bags to the nearest section of seats and collapse. Mental note to self: *Never take books on a trip again.* The train picks up speed. I have no idea what direction we are going, if there are stops along the way, or if this train even goes all the way to Vienna. The only thing I do know is that I walk with angels.

Entranced by the beauty of the countryside, I have no idea that an hour or two had raced by before the train begins to slow to a stop—a stop in the middle of nowhere. No houses. No station. No people. Nothing but countryside. Gorgeous countryside, but *only* countryside. I make no move to get off until the conductor tells me in a tangled mix of German and English that I must.

I muscle my bags to a small cement platform and watch several dozen people walk in various directions into the fields and finally disappear from view. *Hmmm. I wonder where I am?* The train finally chugs away in the direction from which we had come, so I park myself on the small wooden bench. "Interesting," I muse aloud and take an apple and my CD player from my backpack. The quietness and peace is pervasive. Having no clue what to do next, I press play. "Wholly Available" begins and fills my heart.

"Exactly!" I shout to the heavens and stand, raising my hands and singing. "Lord, I've never been more wholly available in my life! Have Your way!" I continue worshiping with the next song, and a delightful shower begins, making the grass glitter with moisture. As the third song begins, God brushes a complete double rainbow from earth to earth right in front of me. Glorious!

I am totally lost, somewhere in Germany, yet totally at home. There is a verse in Matthew that reads something like this: "*. . . lose your life and you'll find it.*" Maybe right here, right now is what that verse means.

Still standing, enveloped in His presence, I am startled when someone taps me on the shoulder. A young woman, with a small bag and a kitty carrier, stands in front of me. "Sophie," she says and points to a pretty black-and-white cat. I touch Sophie's nose with my finger. *Icing on the cake, Lord. I'm somewhere in Germany, and you bring me a kitty. Only You can do this kind of stuff!*

Through somewhat disjointed communication, we introduce ourselves and find out that we are going the same direction. We make our way over a little knoll and take our place on another cement pad with one bench. As we sit, I pet Sophie, and we share a little about our lives.

Together, we board the next train, and the Lord moves us quickly into conversation about Him, about why I am going to Czech as a missionary, about her life in East Germany, about the dreadful years of oppression. She says that she wants to know Jesus, too, so I share a few Scriptures with her, and she asks the Lord to take charge over her life. All of this before the train slows to a stop where she gets off.

Wow, thank You, Lord, for this divine appointment.

The train begins inching forward again. I am still in Germany, as far as I can tell, but I have no idea how far Vienna is. A little fear pops up but is drowned immediately by the reminder *I walk with angels.* "Lord, I can't wait to see what You do next." I laugh and dive into one of my books.

Still engrossed in my book, I barely notice the next stop until I hear wonderful British English. "Hello. May we sit here?"

"Absolutely!" It is so great to hear English. "*Please* sit with me."

Our conversation bursts to life. Diane and her ten-year-old daughter, Beth, are visiting a friend in Vienna and then heading back to their home YWAM base in England where Diane and her husband are on staff! I tell them about my YWAM training in Denver and, instantly, we are kindred spirits.

While talking about mission trips and ministry, we prepare our bags for the stop in Vienna.

"Hey, Kathy, where are you going to stay?" Diane asks.

"I have no clue, really. I think I'll call the YWAM base and see if I can bunk there." But when I can't reach anyone at YWAM, I accept Diane's offer to join them at her friend's house for the night. We hail a taxi and pile in, only to find out that we need a second taxi because we have too much luggage. Three blocks into the trip, our outrageous error becomes perfectly clear. Ten-year-old Beth and I are in one car, Diane is in the other car, and none of us have cell phones. To make matters worse, neither Beth nor I know the address or Diane's friend's name, and we have lost the lead taxi.

We race up and down several streets without success. Our driver knows only a smattering of English, but the one word we all three know is "lost." Totally lost in Vienna, the driver grows angrier by the minute. At one point, he hits the brakes, stops and throws his hands into the air, railing fast in a language that, once again, I am glad I don't understand.

At this point and without hesitation, Beth takes my hands and begins praying: "Lord, we're lost, and we need help. You know where Mom is. Please take us there. Amen."

"Amen," I agree, challenged by her child-like faith.

Our driver mutters something under his breath as he grabs the wheel and starts driving. Vienna is a huge city, and we pass dozens of streets. All of the sudden, however, we see Diane standing on a hilly lane, waving like crazy.

Beth and I high five and holler, "Thank You, Lord!"

Soon after my introduction to Diane's friend, Anna, we all head for bed. I have lost track of how many hours I have been up; I do not know what time it is or even what day it is. I click off the lights, fall into bed, and get the shock of my life. Ghoulish faces all around the room stare holes right through me! I jump up and hit the on switch, which instantly erases the faces. Fear is back in spades! Just as I reach the door knob to get my YWAM buddies, I hear, *I walk with angels* again.

"Okay, Lord," I whisper out loud. "But what now?"

Fear flees. I flip the lights off, and BAM! . . . there they are again. I am kind of hoping angels will come to battle and banish them once and for all, but they don't, so I turn the lights back on. I notice some titles of books cramming the shelves—all demonic "how to" books, and I wonder if Diane knows what her friend is into.

Paul's words about spiritual warfare in Ephesians 6 come to mind. "Okay, Lord," I whisper again. I lay my hands on pictures and posters and cloth tapestries—anything that has a face—commanding them to get out in Jesus' name. I flip the lights back off. They are gone. I fall into bed, peaceful, and completely exhausted.

Morning arrives incredibly quickly. Diane and Beth and I hug good-bye. Anna locks eyes with me, sending a clear message of hate while giving brief directions on how to get to Vienna's train station before leaving for work.

Taking no chances, I decide to leave immediately while her sketchy directions are still fresh in my mind. I drag my heavy suitcase out onto the landing of her third-story apartment, but before I can reach in for my second bag, the door slams shut. I grab the handle. It's locked.

"Well, Lord. It looks like I need a locksmith." I lean back against the wall to wait, quite interested in how He will work things out this time and too tired to think of anything myself. Several minutes pass before I hear someone coming up the steps.

"Hi. Do you speak English?" I ask.

"As a matter of fact, I do," the man answers with a warm smile.

I pour out my story. He listens attentively and, just a little amused, he takes a little tool that's hooked on his key ring, picks the lock, and helps me grab my other two bags.

"You didn't break the lock, did you?"

"Nah, see?" he assures me and tries to open the locked door handle. "Works just fine." He then offers to help me get to the train station. He hails a taxi and, in another language, tells the driver to take me there. I fall into the back seat, turn to thank him, and he is gone. Simply gone.

Yes, I remind myself, *angels rendered service throughout the entire Bible. I know that. But Lord, to me? Again?* Wonder seizes me. Knowing Scriptures and biblical truths is one thing. Living them is quite another thing. A radical thing! An incredibly awesome thing!

I close my eyes and just pour out thanks to Him.

The taxi stops, and we unload my three bags. As I enter the station, a middle-aged gentleman approaches and says, "Here, let me take those for you. They look very heavy."

"Yes, thank you . . . they are heavy, and I'm running out of steam. It feels like I left Colorado a long time ago."

"Hang in there. We have to go to the far side, and there's only one small platform to catch a train to Brno," he explains. "It's easy to miss. I'll take you there."

"Brno," I smile. "I don't have to ask how you knew that."

Our eyes meet, and my heart for my Savior swells. *Lord, I love You.*

Brilliantly painted fast trains are coming and going by the dozens. By the time we reach the far side, however, all I can see is one rusty, decrepit, dark-green train with filthy yellowish-brown windows. It reminds me of trains I have seen in Holocaust movies. What a stark contrast.

The station announces that the train to Brno is leaving. My companion puts my bags in the nearest car and says, "Go with God, Kathy."

We lock eyes again for just a few seconds. "Thank you. I will," and the train chugs to life. In about three hours, hopefully, Hana—my interpreter from the two-week mission trip—will be at the Brno train station to receive me and take me to my new home for as long as the Lord wants me here. Home here, with the Lord, in His care, in His service, and in the charge of His angels.

Letting out a huge sigh, I settle into thoughts of this "homecoming."

Thudding steps interrupt my reverie. A rugged-looking man is racing toward the back of the train. When he reaches my seat, he grabs two of my bags and starts yelling at me in some unfamiliar language.

I yell back, "Hey! Those are mine! You can't take my luggage! Hey!"

But he is not listening. He races through our car and into the next, my bags banging on the seat handles. I grab my backpack and follow him, still screaming, "Hey! Those are *my* bags."

We blast through a few more cars and finally stop in the one next to the engine, where he drops the bags and falls into the nearest seat. I breathlessly fall into the seat across from him and pull my bags closer to me. He grins from ear to ear and says something in Czech, I guess. I am totally confused, but I do manage a weak smile back at him. After all, I do have my bags again.

Just then, the last five cars of the train disconnect, and only the engine and our car head north. This previously dubious man and I finish the ride to Brno. He lifts my bags off the train and hangs around just until he sees a woman approach me. When Hana wraps her arms around me, he smiles and leaves.

It is *so* good to see Hana again. We embrace and chatter while moving my luggage off the platform and onto a sidewalk in front of a run-down building. Not long after that, Hana's husband jumps off a tram and races to meet us. He grabs the luggage and we jog toward another tram. They jump in, and I instantly learn my first valuable lesson about trams and tram drivers. They slam the doors shut whether you're in or only halfway in.

"Ouch!" I squeal and turn a bit crimson as the passengers all have a good giggle at my expense. We bump up and down hills through Brno, the capital of Moravia, the middle section of Czechoslovakia. The tram empties slowly, stop by stop.

"Ours is the next stop, the last one on this line," Hana explains as she prepares to exit. I prepare too—absolutely committed to getting out the door before the driver can catch me again.

Safely out, we head into the woods and up the hillside, each step harder for my weary legs. Once we are finally inside their cozy little home, Hana leads me to my room, unfolds the chair into a bed, and says good-night. I have a much-needed full night's sleep.

At sunrise, Hana knocks on my door, hands me a Czech pastry, and we head out because she has interviews set up for me in several places throughout the city.

I'm stunned by the sights: The castle in the center of Brno, the architecture, the massive transportation system, the throngs of people, and the sheer beauty of the surrounding area. There are deep, dense forests clothed in dark-green moss and filled with climbing ivy and other luscious plants. I look forward to wandering through them once I get settled.

Toward late afternoon this first day, we make our way back to their quiet little village of Omice. Though I never actually live with Hana, I am so at home with her; she is such a dear Christian sister. Over a cup of tea, we discuss the three jobs where I have signed contracts and another five where I will teach English whenever I have free time.

Thrilled with the possibilities ahead of me, I overflow with purpose and with praise that the Lord has gotten me out of that Boston layover and safely into Europe.

Teaching mornings, afternoons, and several night classes take me all over Brno, a huge bustling city, and sometimes into Prague, an even bigger city. I often find myself in need of protection or provision. The Lord never fails me. He made it clear on the plane that I will walk with angels and they are never off-duty.

"AVAILABLE" – FOR DEEPER THOUGHT . . .

1. What opportunity stands before you? Are you taking hold of it or not? Explain.

2. Think about how you stepped out in faith in the past. How did God meet you there?

3. Isaiah has a vision of the Lord on His throne. He's overcome by his own uncleanness and the Lord's forgiveness. In chapter 6, verse 8, he records this: "Then I heard the voice of the Lord, saying, 'Whom shall I send, and who will go for Us?' Then I said, 'Here am I. Send me!'" How does this move you to be more available?

4. Ask the Lord if there is a part for you to play in His Kingdom that perhaps you've not thought of yet. Record the impressions He gives you.

5. "All Scripture is inspired by God and profitable for teaching, for reproof, for correction, for training in righteousness; so that the man of God may be adequate, equipped for every good work" (2 Timothy 3:16–17). How does this encourage you? What steps can you begin to take to become available?

6. "Now may the God of peace . . . equip you in every good thing to do His will, working in us that which is pleasing in His sight, through Jesus Christ, to whom be the glory forever and ever" (Hebrews 13:20–21). Pray this scripture for yourself or for another and write down how it encourages you.

7. Jesus says, "Follow Me, and I will make you fishers of men" (Matthew 4:19). If Jesus equipped fishermen and used them to transform the world, think how He wants to equip and use you. Write your thoughts below.

Available

You are called. You are chosen. To be
My voice, to be My hands.
Whenever I send you, you will go to speak
for me all I command.
Fear not! I am with you. Fear not! You are mine.
Fear not! I have touched you. The words
you speak will be mine.
(Jeremiah 1:4–9; Psalm 22:9–10; Psalm 139:13)

Tender Restoration

With Communism's iron grip broken, restoration rolled across Czechoslovakia like waves of water to the thirsty and dying. And I was there to live it with them as a missionary teaching English. A student of mine, Vaclav, had invited me to spend the weekend in South Moravia with his grandparents, Zdenek and Maruska. Thrilled to host an American, their laughter and smiles bubbled all around me as if my very presence shouted, "Freedom!"

The wine, smooth. The food, delectable. The conversation, animated as this resilient couple beckoned me to participate even in the most intimate details of reclaiming their home and land. Vaclav translated as quickly as possible, but heartfelt warmth transcended any language barrier. We bonded instantly and strongly.

Sweet sleep followed the first full day and gave birth to a glorious morning. While Vaclav visited village friends, Zdenek and I entered the vineyard where he had trod in his youth; his very first steps of redeeming what had been taken and destroyed fifty years earlier. I followed quietly . . . and thoughtfully.

Gentleness defined this little man, a man unencumbered by the bitterness that Communist abuse had carved into so many hearts. I felt honored to spend this day with him. Slowly, soberly we wandered through the wreckage of his once beautiful vineyard while the crisp coolness nipped at our cheeks.

Desolation—row after row of broken, fruitless vines and dry, twisted roots spread before us as we walked. I fought the despair I felt creep into my heart even as I watched this mild-mannered man radiate purpose and passion. Wizened by years of perseverance and weathered by hard work, Zdenek burned with an undying faith that his country would again be free and prosperous, and that he played a vital part in its rebirth.

He fingered every vine, searching every inch for traces of life; caressed every worthless cluster of marble-hard grapes.

I had witnessed the lush vineyards of Western Europe where succulent fruit hung heavily from strong vines. To me, Zdenek's vineyard shouted only harsh tones of hopelessness. His eyes, however, darted to and fro, seeing past the starkness. He held hope for this land, once again his. Possibilities of potential growth lit up his face.

We trudged through weeds and naked vines and finally stumbled upon a dilapidated shed, lying in a heap. Under the splintered boards lay tools, precious tools, testimony of this quiet man's former wealth. A faraway gaze settled over him, like fog rolling into a hushed valley. I wondered if he too had slipped into a time when his youthful enthusiasm could only begin to dream what his fruitful labors would produce. But that was fifty years ago, before Communism had pillaged and raped his country and his people. Now that was over. This was a new time.

Silently, he uncovered a wobbly, three-wheeled cart and set it on its feet. He filled it with a few crudely fashioned tools, some misshapen wooden poles, and several other small items and then began coaxing it over the hard, bumpy earth.

Restoration had begun.

We stopped at a particularly tangled web of vines, and Zdenek seized the rusty old axe with the strength of a much younger man. He stooped, swung the axe, and slashed a clean, long gash in the ground about an inch below the surface. Slash after slash, until hundreds of tiny severed roots dangled freely in the air.

With his every blow, my present gave way to the past and memories surfaced without warning. Alcoholism. Abuse. Betrayal. Bars—gay and straight. Lovers. Shattered hearts and lives. The horrific accident. My brother's casket. Attempted suicide.

Suddenly, Zdenek tapped my shoulder, jolting me back to the present. He spoke no English, but his eyes asked if I was okay. I nodded my head and tried to steady myself. He held my eyes until I nodded a second time, then he went back to work.

More was coming. I knew it. Secrets and dark memories hidden for thirty years were suddenly surfacing. Rattled and scared at what would come next, I forced my attention back toward Zdenek as he began to tend the mangled plant before us.

His wrinkled hands traced the limbs with the severed roots up and over and through the support wires to the trunk of the original vine. There he knelt. Fighting thoughts about *my own* false roots and twisted brokenness, I softly sank to my knees beside him. He slid his hands down the trunk until they came to a ruptured place. Here, split apart, one half of the vine took off to the right. The other part jutted to the left. Life and death hung at this spot. It was here that the milk of the vine had dripped to the hard, unforgiving ground. It was here that the milk had crusted over and hardened, trying desperately to stop the bleeding.

It was here that Zdenek performed his surgery. With a crudely fashioned knife, he cut away the hard, crusty surface and carved both sides of the rupture until fresh new liquid began to ooze. Then he carefully began pressing the two sides together while the newly severed roots wiggled in the air. The two parts, pressed closer together now, surrendered to his touch. He began binding them together with a coarse burlap-type material, beginning well beneath the wound and continuing upward until he reached the fresh, deeper cuts.

Startling me, he placed the wrap in my hands and leaned over the rickety cart, searching for something.

My thoughts drifted back to my brother's death—his mangled bicycle and bloody pajamas. The suffocating pain that God had touched and healed, stopping my bleeding— much like Zdenek's careful work with this damaged vine. My heart warmed at the comparison, as if the Lord were having this humble man act out the precious tender work He had done within me.

Snipping sounds brought my attention back to the task at hand. Zdenek was lopping off the dangling roots, working his way back toward the split trunk. He continued cutting foot after foot of branch after branch until they became too thick to yield to the crude clippers. He cut off the marbled clusters, the dead leaves, and all the wild shoots. He lopped off everything that would steal life from the main source.

Freed from all that weight, Zdenek knelt again and pressed the left and right sides completely together until the precious liquid stopped oozing. Then he motioned for me to continue the wrapping. Layer upon layer, I tightly and resolutely covered the cut, sealing the life-giving liquid inside, protecting the freshly opened wound so that it could heal and once again send out new branches to bear much fruit.

Oh, my Lord, for that to be true, I thought, for this vineyard and for me. *Lord, you've healed such a deep wound, but there are still others that seep, You know. The drinking . . . the abuse . . . Oh, Lor...*

"Katka?"

Looking up, I smiled at Zdenek's use of the Czech name for Kathy and flipped away a few tears that had leaked out. He motioned for me keep pressure on two sides while he began strategically placing the odd poles under what remained of the two branches to support them and to remove all pressure from the "sutured" rupture. Pleased, he broke into a soft grin. Taking the wrap from me, he tied it off and cut it. Then he took something like a paintbrush and some pink pasty goo and totally soaked and sealed the once ruptured area. Zdenek then turned and touched a remaining tear clinging to my cheek and whispered something in Czech. We had no common words, but we shared the vocabulary of the heart, which was more than enough.

It surprised me when he took the axe again and started working the sliced earth where shallow roots had taken sustenance for so long. I thought we had finished, but he knew we hadn't. Feverishly, he sliced the ground, deeper and deeper. The brittle tendrils of a much larger root reluctantly gave in to the blows. Zdenek tossed the worthless root into the cart, clapped, and laughed from his toes. A victory won. His gentle eyes twinkled with hope and expectation. As he urged the old cart to the next vine, I gazed at the artificially supported grapevine. To me, the vine seemed to have so little chance of recovery.

Relentlessly, the past exploded into the present. Like a motion picture, I saw the horrible fights when Dad came home drunk, using fists and boots for words; the nights of hiding in my big brother Eddy's room for safety; Eddy's terrible accident; the escape I found in sports and drinking and homosexual relationships; and my suicide attempt. Just like the vines— broken and desolate. But . . . but alive!

This radically altered vine still had life-sustaining liquid running in its limbs, and I still had blood coursing through my veins. Despite so many personal false roots and ruptures, here I stood, in this precious country, with these amazing people, the Lord Himself opening the door for me to teach here and do missionary work. Just as Zdenek wasn't discouraged or done, neither was my Lord. Hope rose within me.

We worked until the sun began to set and then quietly padded our way through the vineyard—back to this man's small but precious house—*his* house once again. We ate a simple meal in soft silence, pleased with a day well lived.

I slipped between the sheets, a cautious expectation easing into my heart where all those dark flashbacks had hidden. Zdenek believed his vineyard would thrive again. Perhaps, I would too.

Just after the sun peeked over the horizon, we shared a small breakfast, and I hugged this sweet family good-bye. Zdenek and Vaclav headed to the vineyard, and I boarded the rusty green train that would carry me back to Brno and toward my future. As I traveled the countryside, my heart pounded with questions, hopes, and doubts. I knew that Zdenek would bring abundance where there had been ruin and death. His tools? Sharp. Crude. Unrelenting. But directed by love, by a passion to restore.

As the tired train rattled over the uneven tracks, I better understood *real* grace; its tools were like teeth that cut and bit and severed and pruned. My Lord Jesus wanted passionately to redeem and restore, to replace barrenness with fruitfulness, hopelessness with expectancy, and pain with healing. True restoration. Soothed by the rhythmic rocking of the train, I smiled much like Zdenek had as he envisioned what would come from his labor. No less would my Lord deal with my false roots and with the twisted, buried parts of my life.

I pondered the total love in Zdenek's wrinkled hands as he first assessed the damage and set about his work. My restoration rested in the nailed-scarred hands of Love Himself, and at just that moment He brought Deuteronomy 29:18 to my mind, "that there will not be among you a root bearing poisonous fruit . . ."

I bent forward, as there wasn't room to kneel. "Lord, axe the root out of me, please. Whatever it is, get it," I whispered to Him. "I don't want to keep chopping off bad fruit, Lord. Please get it."

It took Zdenek about thirty minutes to axe the dead root out of that first vine, his love for his vineyard and its fruitfulness clear. How long it would take my Lord, I had no clue, but this I knew: His heart was in the pruning. It was a heart of perfect love cutting away whatever would hinder fruitful, abundant life for me.

Sweet phrases from Jesus's words in John 15 filled my mind. *I am the true vine, and My Father is the vinedresser. Abide in me, be pruned, and you will bear much fruit. My Father is glorified when you bear much fruit and prove to be My disciple.*

"Amen, my Lord. Prune away. I am Yours."

"TENDER RESTORATION" –
FOR DEEPER THOUGHT . . .

1. Has your present ever been interrupted by memories from your past? How did you deal with the interruption?

2. Is there a memory that has surfaced more than once that may need dealt with in some detail? Explain.

3. If it is a bad memory, what can you do to "redeem" it or receive some healing if it still hurts?

4. What have you lost that you would like to restore? A hope? A relationship? What is the first step in this restoration process?

5. Is there a situation in your life that seems totally ruined or hopeless? How could you begin to bring life and hope into that situation?

6. In Joel 2:13, the Lord urges Israel to turn to Him because He is compassionate, slow to anger, abounding in loving-kindness, and in verse 25 He promises that He will restore all the years the locusts had eaten. What would you like the Lord to restore in your life? How can you cooperate with Him in this restoration process?

7. Matthew 3:10 says, "The axe is already laid at the root of the trees; therefore, every tree that does not bear good fruit is cut down and thrown into the fire." What kind of fruit are you bearing? How willing are you to let the Lord axe out the bad roots and fruits so that you can bear more good fruit?

Tender Restoration

After you have suffered for a little while,
The God of all grace who calls you His
child will Himself lift you up.
He will strengthen; He will comfort; He will
establish; He will confirm.
And you will be gold.
(1 Peter 5:10)

Barefoot

When I could no longer play sports, which I loved and which had lured me back into college, I settled into a career as a teacher and spent twenty-five years in the middle school English classroom, where I found that I loved teaching as much as I loved playing sports. So when the door opened into the former Eastern European country of Czechoslovakia in 1989, I jumped at the chance to teach English and enter into full-time ministry there.

After a few months of caring for my Grandma back in the States, I was back "home" in Brno with the people I had come to love dearly. I resumed many of my previous teaching jobs, and other doors opened.

I taught at a secondary school, at the music university in Brno, at the Salvation Army facility, and at a nursing school. I also held several evening classes for various groups of people who were eager to learn English.

I spent weekends traveling with students, meeting families, "becoming" family. We explored incredible castles and cathedrals and other architectural wonders throughout the country. I sat in world-famous concert halls listening to magnificent symphonies performed by my very own students. I spent rich time in hospitals playing the guitar and singing with kids who were battling cancer due to the fallout of Chernobyl. I traveled with pastors to remote villages to pray with families, and over the course of two-plus years, I made many lifelong friendships.

Consistently stretched by language and travel challenges, I felt alert and blessed. The excitement and depth of it all fed the inner drive that my former sports competition had once satisfied. Truly, my heart had found a home. The Mikolov family took me in as one of their own, and I instantly loved them all: Jirina, her husband, Michal, and their son, Bohos. They all spoke English well, so our conversations were full and easy. In addition, Jirina and I began teaching English classes together and hosting an evening prayer meeting. They owned a beautiful house, which actually shocked me because the Communists had taken almost everything and left the rest in despicable disrepair. I called their home my castle. It was about three miles from Biskupi Gymnasium, a strongly academic prep school, where I taught English four periods a day.

Trams and buses ran every ten minutes between school and home, and I often had to hop one for the sake of time. However, when time didn't matter, I took the skinny dirt path that wound like a thin ribbon through the woods.

One particular Saturday, as the first soft rays of sunlight drifted into my room, I decided to head into the woods. I stuffed my backpack with my Bible, concordance, and several books to read and study. My plan was to *capture* the third bench on the second turn of the path before anyone else could claim it and then to study, read, and prepare for Sunday morning. I had been invited to speak at a friend's church and wanted very much to be ready.

I swung the bulging pack—heavier than was healthy, I'm sure—onto my back and marched into the woods, as if on a secret mission. Bent over and intent on capturing that bench, I glued my eyes to the path, oblivious to everything around me. Ideas for Sunday's message bounced back and forth in my brain, and a battle plan quickly took shape as I evaluated each idea. By the time I reached the bench, I knew exactly where to begin reading, how to begin structuring the message, and where to find the supporting material to drive the message home.

"Yes!" I shouted as I turned the corner and spied my bench. I picked up my pace and took ownership by spreading books from end to end, leaving a small place for me to sit right in the middle. Then I dove in—Bible open, study notes accessible, support materials within reach, brain engaged, and pen flying across blank sheets of paper. Focused and busy—life at its best.

And it lasted about ten minutes. My single-mindedness vaporized. Just like that. Gone! I couldn't even concentrate enough to put one sentence together.

Like bubbles rising from deep waters, something was fighting its way to the surface. A thought? An idea? An invitation? I wasn't sure. I couldn't quite make it out. I shook my head as if to clear cobwebs and resolutely headed back into doing what needed done. Studying. Writing. Preparing.

But mysterious internal interruptions kept pressing toward the surface again and again until I finally slammed my books shut, re-stuffed my backpack, and dropped into a slouch of surrender, totally exasperated. No matter what I did, I couldn't quiet the inner rumblings, so I decided to stop fighting them.

Abandoning *my* plans, I tried to open my mind to what was bubbling.

Come walk barefoot with me.

"Huh?" I blurted out loud. "That makes *no* sense."

I hadn't been barefooted since the day I was born. In fact, my feet had quite a history—corrective shoes at three years old, three surgeries, bones sawn in two and realigned and secured with screws, and every kind of orthotics conceived by man. Only one word described my feet—painful. Mom almost had to hog-tie me to get my shoes off at bedtime because their constant support kept the pain manageable.

So, walk barefoot? No way!

Come—walk barefoot with Me.

The impression was more distinct this time. The pause after the "Come" quickened me somehow . . . as if deep had just called to deep. I also sensed an emphasis on "Me." Barefoot didn't make any sense in the natural world, but spiritual things can never be understood with reason, so I quieted my mind to allow my spirit to respond.

Come . . . walk barefoot . . . with Me.

The third time. Patient but insistent. Clear.

After all, I pondered, I *had* come to Eastern Europe because the Lord had so powerfully opened the door for me. I *had* come at His bidding, to do His work, to serve Him. I *had* come to listen and obey as best as I could.

My thoughts drifted to 1 Samuel 3. The Lord called young Samuel three times. Each time he ran to Eli to see what he wanted. Finally, Eli perceived that it was the Lord who was beckoning the boy, so he told Samuel that if he heard the voice again, he should respond, "Speak LORD, for Your servant is listening" (1 Samuel 3:10).

There it stood—a warm invitation. A summons of sorts, coaxing me to come.

"Yes, Lord, I hear You," I whispered as I bent over, removed my tennis shoes, and slipped off my socks. I chuckled at my bright-white feet, in comical contrast with my dark, suntanned legs. Lightness floated through my spirit. I sensed His smile, His delight. His presence was strong as I headed deeper into the woods with Him, barefoot, scars from the surgeries zigzagging across the tops of my feet.

The path stretched before me like a chocolate-brown ribbon, winding here and there, aimlessly, easily, freely . . . inviting me to play, to indulge, to let go. Strangely, somehow I knew that I needed to pocket my watch. Time mattered not, almost as if it had been suspended altogether.

With each step, my senses intensified. I had expected pain, walking barefoot, but the coolness of the soft, moist dirt seemed to send small delightful darts of energy into my feet, startling and wonderful. I lingered, allowing the gentle sensation to massage my feet, one toe at a time, taking it in, relishing each little burst. As it moved toward my heels, I giggled—not as if tickled but as if enlivened—as if the darts were ministering healing somehow. I tarried, inviting it to travel through my feet, up through my body, into my head; I was totally immersed *in* the moment.

Suddenly, my determined march through the woods, up the path to the bench, and to my work flashed in my memory. I laughed right out loud—a long, hearty laugh, a laugh that bounced off the rocks and trees and soft earth and came back rich and magnified—as if the Lord Himself and His creation laughed with me. A laughter from a long-forgotten place.

When had I lost laughter? It was faintly familiar but from a faraway, dimly lit past. It was as if the laughter had been a giant bubble, longing to be heard, finally bursting to the surface, breaking through the hard years that had silenced it.

As the playful darts subsided, my nose quickly caught the earthy smell of the soft soil . . . rich and fertile, ready to receive seed and render a harvest. I saw myself, decades ago, on my brother-in-law's tractor, plowing, watching the seagulls dive down to pick out worms from the shiny slabs of freshly cut earth, relishing the smell—the full, rich scent of moist earth.

I meandered from side to side on the path, finding little muddy puddles, pressing my feet into the goo, feeling it ooze between my toes, tickling them, chilling them; I chuckled unabashedly like a child at play.

Come. Walk barefoot with Me.

"Never have I walked barefoot in the mud, Lord, never." I exclaimed like a boisterous six-year-old. "Oh, I should have been doing this all along."

I know, He whispered to my spirit, and I could almost see the loving smile spreading across His face as He watched me— His child—enjoy His creation as never before.

When the path turned green with deep, dense moss, I hop-scotched my imaginary chalk-drawn pattern up and back, up and back, the mossy cushion tenderly receiving my feet and then releasing them with a spring, like a spongy trampoline, each bounce bringing a sense of renewal somehow, restoration.

The smell changed dramatically . . . fragrant and sweet, almost perfumed. It enticed me to breathe deeply, to fill myself with its gift. Alive. Breathlessly alive.

We ambled deeper into the forest, where the thick succulent moss clothed gigantic trees as with regal robes, elegant beyond imagination. They stood at attention like soldiers, welcoming their King, their limbs saluting, their branches blocking most of the sunlight, forming living canopies of shelter and safety, of peace and comfort.

Gradually, an overwhelming awareness of protection blanketed me, like when Grandma B. would pull one of her handmade heavy quilts up under my chin and around my shoulders. I felt loved and safely tucked in. I stopped to take it in. It embraced me. Held me.

Profound silence. Perfect stillness.

I will never leave you nor forsake you, resonated in my soul. I had read and heard those words many times, but not like this. The Lord *gave* them to *me* this time. He imprinted them on my heart with His nail-scarred hands. I closed my eyes as this profound interaction with the Almighty bathed my type-A, over-achieving nature, transforming it, conforming it, moving it aside, making more room for *His* nature.

"Lord, please saturate me with this truth," I whispered.

When I finally opened my eyes, three thin shafts of sunlight had found their way through the overhead canopy of greens, turning the moisture in the air into thousands of twinkling, dancing dots of color. A kaleidoscope of colors. The grandest rainbow I had ever seen flashed in my memory, but here, hundreds of colors, breathtaking variations of colors, mixed together. Had He taken scales from my eyes, or were these revelations reserved for supernatural times—for *barefoot times*?

The intricacy of the luscious filter that allowed in the columns of light filled my senses now. A variation of vines filled empty spaces like fragile lace, weaving around and under and through branches, multitudes of greens melting into one another, blending, harmonizing perfectly with the strong green leaves of the straight, tall trees as they stretched and reached for the heavens.

Vines hung from the rafters above, begging me to run and swing like Tarzan, to let them pull me through space, joining the dance of the colors. Unrestrained freedom. Unabashed laughter. *Jesus and I . . . Oh, my precious Lord . . .* breaking through the shafts of light as if through thin, cleansing waterfalls. Breathless. *Oh, my precious Lord. Who could have imagined?*

Slowing to a stop, exhilarated, I suddenly noticed the vine's large pointed leaves. Complex vein-like patterns filled each one. No geometry class on earth could account for such perfectly detailed shapes. Delicate vines fell to the ground, as well, each covered with soft short fuzz tingling my fingertips.

For a brief second, I wondered if I was dreaming. I wondered if this was real. But then the narrow path caught my eye again. It called me deeper, and I responded. The landscape on my left slowly changed, as the brown and green of earth and trees gave way to rocks of all sizes and colors. Staggering colors. New colors. Brownish oranges and golden greens and greenish yellows. Enthralled, I looked closer. Lichen! Dozens of different kinds. It was startling, a tapestry transforming these rocks into beings artistically, majestically clothed by the Master Designer, the Creator Himself. Coverings not ever woven or even imagined by man. Beyond us. Higher than our highest thoughts.

A gentle gurgling sound caught my attention, and I turned toward it. A tiny track of water was winding its way through the crevices between and behind the rocks. As if playing hide 'n seek, sometimes it trickled over a rock but then quickly ducked behind it again, giggling as it went, carefree and playful, totally uninhibited.

As if on cue, other new sounds emerged as instruments in an orchestra building toward crescendo, a symphony of sound. Surround sound. Beyond surround sound. One by one, the song of each bird found my ears and soon blended into the perfect unity of innumerable birds and songs. Then the songs of other little creatures merged. The ones in the water, the ones on the earth, the ones on the moss and in the lichen and near the rocks joined the opus. Many voices. Scales and scales of notes, new notes. Complicated cadences, hundreds of melodies. Creation singing.

Even the rocks will cry out if we don't praise Him. I smiled at Jesus's words in Luke 19. Music filled the air, catching my spirit, lifting it higher and wider and deeper, dancing to creation's cantata, twirling with the thousands of little colors in a shaft of sunlight now covering me, bringing warm waves of love and contentment.

The *Son.* With me. In me. Together and complete. One.

I settled on a stump of wood, listening with my entire being, opening myself entirely to my Lord. *Come to Me when you are thirsty and drink . . . rivers of living water will flow from your heart . . . I am that living water . . . I will flow through you . . . you will never thirst again . . . let Me be your all in all.*

Surrendered. Abandoned. Available. Effortlessly walking barefoot with my Lord, the lover of my soul. I slid to my knees, lifted my head, gazed into that beam of light, and poured out my heart. "Yes, my Lord. Please help me grasp all that You are doing and saying right now. I *so* want to *know* You and Your ways. You only did what You saw the Father doing. The ease and grace and pace of Your life must be mine, as You pour me out as You please. I came to Eastern Europe to *do.* You are urging me to *be.* To be one *with* You, not do *for* You. To minister *to* You, not *for* You. To be enraptured *with* You in passionate love, not entrapped in feverish work *for* You."

I hardly remember leaving that spot of communion, and I have no recollection of what time it was, but eventually I reached the bench, smiled at the change of plans, swung my backpack over a shoulder, and headed home. A life-changing exchange had taken place in those woods on that day. I traded relentless *doing* for contented *being,* and He began accomplishing *His* work through me—out of relationship with Him.

I did share a message that Sunday, about the glory and love of God that melts hearts and heals wounds. It wasn't a message hammered out by my own ideas and skill and study and work. It was a message first lived with Him in the woods and then shared effortlessly from my heart, not my head.

As Jesus walked this earth, He easily shared God's heart because He communed with His Father and knew His Father's heart. Everything Jesus said or did came out of His intimate love relationship with His Father. How much more must it be us? Only as we *become* the message, can we *give* the message.

His invitation still beckons, *Come. Walk barefoot with Me.*

"BAREFOOT" – FOR DEEPER THOUGHT . . .

1. How often are you so focused on what you think needs done, and done your way, that you leave very little room for creative alternatives? What are some examples?

2. Proverbs 16:9 tells us that "The mind of man plans his way, but the Lord directs his steps." What comes to your mind as you read this verse? What steps can you take to become more receptive to the Lord directing your steps?

3. How receptive are you to internal nudges to take a different course of action when yours is not working? How can you tell if these "nudges" are from God? What steps will you take to be more receptive?

4. 1 Samuel 3 tells the story of a very receptive little boy. During the night, Samuel heard his name being called three times. Eli, the high priest, told Samuel how to respond the next time by saying, "Speak, Lord, for your servant is listening." God speaks in many ways: Through His Word, devotionals, books, fellow believers, worship, nature. How accustomed are you to sensing His desire to converse with you?

5. In 1 Kings 19, the prophet Elijah is in a crisis, running for his life. God tells him to go stand on the mountain before Him. As the LORD passes by, there is a tornadic wind, an earthquake, and a fire, but God is not in any of these. Then Elijah hears a still, small voice like a gentle whisper. It is the Lord engaging him in conversation. How does God communicate with you? In a crisis, or in a culture where busyness is the dominant description of how we live, how do you find time to be quiet and listen to that still, small voice? How do you think your life would change if you made time to be still and listen to however He wishes to communicate with you?

6. Describe what a "barefoot time" with the Lord would be like for you. How do you think it would change your day? If you did it once a month, how would it change your year?

Barefoot

In the secret place of the most high God, that's
where His whisper comes.
In the secret place of the most high God, when
the heart is still and the mind is at rest,
Hidden in the shadow of His wings.
Safe within that secret place.
(Psalms 25:14, 31:20, 91:1, 17:8)

Part Two

Eyeballs

Danny is famous. And what can possibly be better than being famous? Star athletes, actors, and actresses quickly come to mind. Visions of their mansions, exotic clothes, foreign cars, and travels dance in our imaginations. The power and pull of famous people push our fantasies far beyond where we live our own day-to-day, ordinary, even humdrum, lives. Ahhhh, to be famous—even if only for a day.

But Danny is now a seventh-grader at my school. I know about him from last year and have discovered that being famous in middle school can mean several things—most of which are bad. For Danny, *everything* that makes him famous is bad.

First of all, in sixth grade he became intimately acquainted with the front office staff and the assistant principal, you know, the person in charge of discipline. Never a good thing.

Secondly, all the teachers here are well aware of Danny's reputation and dread finding his name on their roll sheets. Not that he is the worst kid in the school, but let's just say he is certainly a handful.

Furthermore, the *labels* flash in neon lights. Now we educators would rather die than even whisper the word, but "labeling" happens at all grade levels, no matter how cleverly it is disguised. The primary kiddos have cutesy group names like the Blue Birds, Red Birds, and Yellow Birds. In third, fourth, and fifth grade, cutesy doesn't cut it, so teachers use creative group names like Lions, Tigers, and Bears. As middle school teachers, our educational acumen is really stretched, so we create acronyms: ADD, ESL, OCD, ADHD, SPED, ILP, and the list goes on and on.

But now Danny is about to begin seventh grade with files—covered with the alphabet following his name—all stuffed into a personal folder that is the fattest one in the filing cabinet. Another not-so-good sign.

So, as the first day of the new school year inches closer, thoughts of Danny escalate dramatically as we set up our classrooms and prepare for that tough first week, packed with the indescribably delightful chaos of greeting over six hundred middle school students. If their undiluted energy could be bottled, the energy crisis would vanish.

On the last day of preparation, the hallway speakers finally crackle with Pam's official front office voice, "Teachers. Your rosters are in your mailboxes. Pick them up at your leisure." I laugh out loud. *Leisure? It is more like the seventh-grade lunch rush.* I join the forty-eight teachers who scurry into the halls and cram into the closet-sized office space that holds our mailboxes and those precious roll sheets. Calling out names, passing packets over heads and through the open-ended boxes, one by one, we grab our sheets, scanning them like high-speed lasers. Sighs of huge relief, various gasps of "oh, no" and a few other words that can't be shared fill the air.

Sure enough, in my first period reading class, right there in black and white, I spot Danny's name. All kinds of thoughts bounce around as I head toward my classroom. In one long, slow breath, I lift my eyes and whisper, "Oh, Lord. Help!"

Ms. Paxt, Danny's personal aide, and the principal run me down and give me a forty-second briefing on what each of Danny's acronyms means, what I can and can't expect from him in the classroom, and ask if I can handle it.

"Well, of course," I retort. After all, I'm an experienced teacher, and I thrive on challenges. My thoughts drift to the years I taught in Czech and Mexico—wonderful and challenging. My heart smiles, thinking of the various middle schools where I've taught, and my time at CSU . . . so many great memories.

What Ms. Paxt and the principal fail to add is that seven other students in this class also have various letters behind their names and that a few others are only reading at the third-grade level. Thus, another school year begins.

On day one of seventh grade, Danny is taller than even the eighth graders and skinnier than most. And, as if to prove that he doesn't fit anywhere, his *daily* garb is an XXL Bronco jersey and his cool Bronco hat, cocked down and to the side, always covering half of his face so that only one eye is visible.

Danny's final claim to fame is the worst of all—that full-time personal aide. Ms. Paxt has shadowed Danny every minute of every school day for several years now, as if attached to him by a bungee cord. Even outside the boys' bathroom, she stands as a sentry, waiting, listening, and counting seconds by her watch.

No educational spin can erase Danny's fame, and he "gets it." He *knows* he doesn't belong, and acts accordingly. I watch as he silently shuffles to and from class in his oversized jersey with his head lowered and his body bent forward, totally alienated from the hundreds of kids bustling all around him. I can't help but see that his entire demeanor and attire hang like black shrouds of shame—his life and labels just too heavy a burden.

That's Danny. Quietly combustible, living on the thinnest edge of life.

And . . . famous.

Day one passes quickly, and I enthusiastically jump into day two. Things are going very smoothly until something triggers Danny. He's about to blow. Some of the kids around him are getting wound up like tight, tiny springs, and I'm on the other side of the classroom.

Trying not to alarm the rest of the students, I do the first thing that hits my brain. I smack the book in my hand on the nearest desk, nearly causing the little blond girl in that seat to faint. But it grabs the attention of all, including Ms. Paxt. I jerk my head toward the door as her hint to hustle Danny into the hall before we are left with just pieces to pick up. Minutes later, the bell rings, and we've survived the second day—barely.

On day three, I intercept Danny and Ms. Paxt before they get to the classroom, and we make an emergency plan. Danny decides that he will adjust the bill of his cap when he first begins to burst, and whether I notice it or not, he may leave the room—with his aide, of course.

The bell rings, and the rest of my twenty-nine students tumble into the room like spilled marbles. While bouncing from friend to friend, as if allergic to their seats, I'm thinking of using the "book slap" again. I purposely avoid the shy little blond from yesterday and smack the desk of the fastest chatterer instead.

"Take your seats, please, and eyeballs, class. Eyeballs. Right up here. Glued to mine." I shoot them my "teacher" look.

(I always use it the first week or so.) "I want all sixty eyeballs right here, right now."

Well, fifty-nine. Half of Danny's face is always safely hidden behind his ball cap. I don't want him to lift the brim and blow, but I am curious why he pulls one side down so low. Maybe Danny thinks it's the "cool" look, or in his case, the "tough" look. Immediately, I toss candy to the five or six kids who are sitting quietly, looking at me.

By the fourth day, I toss candy to about half the class. By Tuesday of the second week, I toss treats to the entire group. Now that the dear ones know how to come in, sit down, be quiet, and look at me, I can actually get to really know the kids and begin teaching.

Week three begins, and I start wearing my own sports paraphernalia—to reach Danny and because I'm a sports fanatic myself. I am totally jazzed when he notices and comments on my Broncos shirt. We've connected!

But I'm a tad alarmed on Tuesday when Danny pops into the classroom before the bell, *without* Ms. Paxt. I mean, she usually intercepts him the second he crosses the school's threshold.

"Hey, did you watch the Broncos last night?" he blurts, and we're off—talking sports a mile a minute. Ms. Paxt bursts through the door, ready to bandage any damage, and mouths, "I am sorry," wrinkles of distress folding her face. My thumbs up disarms her, and she slips into the nearest desk, listening to more football stats than she ever wanted to know. I don't think she has ever seen this side of Danny.

After another week, he's coming to my room twenty minutes before school starts just to hang out, talk sports, and get some help with his work. At midterm, Ms. Paxt no longer accompanies him to and through first period. He is all mine. And I am thrilled. Our one-on-one time before school is a lifeline for this defeated seventh-grader.

Week five? He seldom moves the brim of his hat now, and if he does, I instantly get a sports example or analogy into the flow of my instruction to help him avert a collapse. Just as quickly, he releases his hat, looks up, and smiles, confidence shining in his eye. He's still hiding, but he's getting stronger. Getting braver. When hearts are in sync in a classroom, lives are changed, and Danny and I are right there. It is the sweetest place I know.

During the following weeks, Danny begins inching his hand into the air to ask and answer questions. All of those letters behind his name? They are only symbols of some hard times, some deep hurts, and experiences quite foreign to most seventh-graders. There is a depth to Danny, and it shows as he warily begins to communicate. He is "tall" beyond his years, more mature than the other kids, and they notice it. Bonds form. Kids ask to be his partner. He begins to trust. He begins to fit. He was opening up, like a tight rosebud slowly surrendering to warmth and light.

We are all in a rhythm now that makes a classroom buzz and hum with energy. We are comfortable with each other. I don't need to begin each class with, "Eyeballs up here," because the kids say it now.

Then *bam!* Just before the end of first quarter, it happens.

Danny's hand jerks up to his hat. I quickly comment on the Bronco's last game and sputter some imaginary statistics, hoping it will save him. But this time he doesn't respond. I begin moving quickly to his side. Kids begin tensing and squirming, their heads jerking around to watch Danny. I'm losing them.

"Eyeballs, class. Eyeballs right up here! Now!" I shout.

In a flash, Danny knocks his hat off and with one finger, pops his hidden eyeball right out of its socket. It bounces and then rolls around on his desk!

The girls fly out of their seats and jump in all directions. Their squeals hit the ceiling, "Yuck! Ew! Gross!" The boys come unglued, too, and holler, "Cool! Lemesee! Awesome, dude!" The girls race to the far corner of the room. The boys swarm Danny, grubby hands grabbing for his eyeball.

I . . . well . . . I . . . um . . . I just stand there. I can't find one word to say. Danny has accomplished the miraculous—rendering a Language Arts teacher speechless. I don't know how much time elapses. I don't realize how loud we are. I myself am vacillating between "Wow" and "Ew."

Then Danny sneaks me a peek with his intact eye, and the smile that erupts on his face floods me with emotion. He had flipped his hidden eyeball out on purpose! He had bravely exposed his hidden dark secret, the very source of his shame.

Ohmygosh! This wasn't a meltdown at all. My heart is thumping wildly. *What an incredible risk Danny just took! Oh, my Lord! Don't let this backfire. Please! Oh, Lord! Help me handle this well! They sure didn't cover THIS in my college Methods of Teaching classes.*

I gather my scattered senses and manage to finally calm the girls down and re-glue the boys to their seats. I send Danny to the restroom to wash the thing off before he sticks it back in place. Naturally, I consent and let him put it back in place in front of the class so that all who care to watch can. Only a few girls squeak, "Ew," and peek through their fingers.

Danny stands comfortably next to my desk and replaces his eyeball. He explains how and when he lost his eye and how many eyeballs and colors he has chosen over the years. He is talking with peers as if it's always been a natural thing to do. Showing his heart and sharing his life with an easy, smooth freedom. How far he has come. I am overwhelmed and begin blinking back tears.

Well, by fourth period, I'm now famous, too. The halls are buzzing. The energy in the locker bays has doubled. Nearly six hundred kids are bouncing like tight rubber balls, wanting Danny to do it again. This is *the* happening of the quarter . . . maybe of the year.

After sixth period, I spy Danny at the end of the hall. He's in his gym T-shirt, not his super large Bronco jersey, his hat is straight, his smile warm and alive. He is joking and laughing with the kids in his locker bay, and the labels behind his name? Evaporating with each laugh, with each high five, with each pat on the back.

As I watch, quiet echoes of a declaration God made to Joshua thousands of years ago reach my heart. *Today I have rolled away your reproach and shame. Be strong. Be very courageous.*

"Rolled away" certainly has a new ring to it now, and I can imagine heaven chuckling right along with me. Yet beyond the humor is a tall, skinny kid who brought what was hidden to the light and reminded me of something crucial. Danny loosed the thing that had held him captive and found freedom and acceptance.

Shrouds of shame vanish for anyone willing to make them visible to Jesus, the Lord of Light.

Be strong, Danny. Be very courageous.

"EYEBALLS" – FOR DEEPER THOUGHT . . .

1. Do you know a "Danny"? Someone who doesn't fit in? Someone who tends to hide? How can you come alongside and encourage him/her? What can you do to love that person back to life?

2. Are you a "Danny?" Do you feel like you don't fit and/or are fighting shame? What steps can you take to overcome?

3. Do you tend to criticize those who may be a little odd or different? Do you shy away from them, or do you tend to empathize with them and help them? What would you like to do differently the next time you meet a "Danny"?

4. God used Moses to lead Israel out of Egypt and into the Promised Land. What an amazing day it must have been for them in Joshua 5:9 where the LORD told Joshua, "Today I have rolled away the reproach of Egypt from you." What steps can you take to rid yourself or someone else of shame?

5. It is risky to let others see into our lives, but what will you gain if you're honest about the things that darken your days?

6. Isaiah 1:18 says, "'Come now, and let us reason together,' says the Lord, 'Though your sins are as scarlet, they will be as white as snow; Though they are red like crimson, they will be like wool.'" How does this encourage you to let the Lord deal with your shame?

7. 1 John 1:9 tells us that "If we confess our sins, He is faithful and righteous to forgive us our sins and to cleanse us from all unrighteousness." Even if we're ashamed of something someone else did to us, Jesus can and will cleanse us when we open ourselves to Him and His work. What do you need to confess?

Eyeballs

I stand before Your throne, clothed
in filthy rags.
Satan stands there at my right hand,
accusing me—pointing out all my sin.
"I rebuke you," says the angel of the Lord.
"This is one that I've plucked from the fire.
Remove the filthy garments and clothe
him with festive robes."
(Zechariah 3:1–5)

Empty Pockets

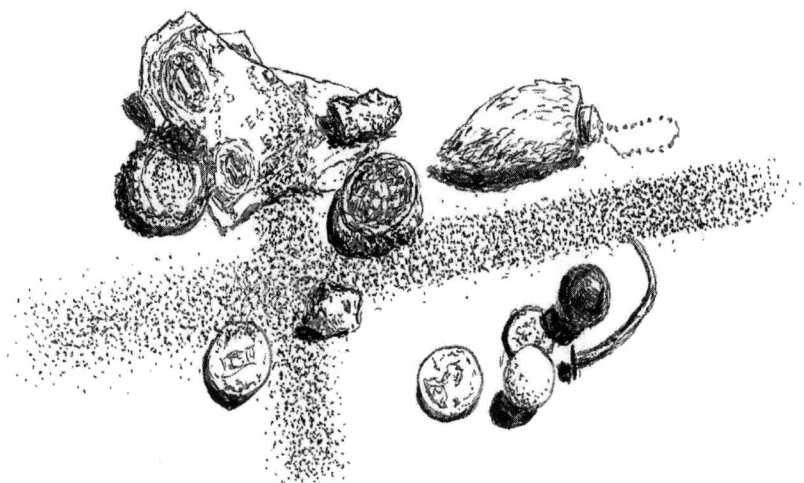

Okay. My first thought when I hear those two words? Thousands of statically charged tissue shreds clutching every piece of clothing in the dryer because no one in my house believes in empty pockets! My second thought? The money—"tips" as I call them—innocently coaxed out of pockets by every agitation of the washing machine. And be they green or be they silver, they be mine and are quickly plunked into my "mad money" jar hidden in the deep recesses of my top dresser drawer. Ahhhh, yes, those tips that eventually pay for a double burger and small fry. I mean, what else can I say? Nothing really, that is, until a young man named Nate suddenly, urgently, redefined "empty pockets" forever.

You know the type. Some of you have seventh-grade sons like Nate. You exhale loudly when they leave for school in the morning and then cross your fingers as they reenter. Loud. Energetic. Annoying. Fun. Accidents waiting to happen, with smiles that melt your heart yet tempt you to tear your hair out . . . or theirs.

Nate's entrance into my classroom was preceded by his reputation. As a teacher, I saw his file stuffed with notes from several elementary teachers, but one note in particular caught my eye. "Nate is great, but if it's possible to be ADHHHHHD, Nate is that. He's a little wild man."

Now, I had taught several kids diagnosed with Attention Deficit Hyperactivity Disorder, but I had never seen it written with five H's. I *knew* that I would need every skill I'd ever learned and then some, so I had several interventions in place on Nate's first day. He needed every one of them, and we instantly began inventing more. But I liked him and understood why that teacher with the five H's had said he was a great kid.

However, as our school's yearly mission trip neared, I could hardly imagine how nine days in Juarez, Mexico, would be with Nate. I have to admit that I secretly began brainstorming all the reasons why Nate should *not* accompany us. They were logical, reasonable, and solidly sane, yet they waged war with my heart. My only hope was that this little wild man would not want to go, if for no other reason than to do the exact opposite of what his pastor dad wanted him to do.

But sure enough. Nate was the first student to sign up. Hear the parental colossal exhale? Now, I was no rookie. I had co-led many mission trips to Juarez accompanied by seventh-graders. What could Nate do? I mean, really?

Departure day arrived, and the five leaders boarded the bus first to find our strategically chosen seats to wait for the stampede. Parents barely squeaked out their good-byes before sons and daughters began bolting for their own carefully chosen seats.

The old, tired bus began chugging south, and we started counting victories in small milestones, like leaving at 4:00 a.m.

as planned and not two hours later; and completing the first bathroom break in under an hour; and traveling four hours without a bus break down.

I guess an eighteen-hour bus ride with middle schoolers could cause the skin to prickle with nightmarish goose bumps, but when your heart beats with kids this age, eighteen hours is a gift of laughter and challenge and adventure. Their energy causes the hair to stand up straight and the heart to thump with possibilities. With Nate added to the mix, I suddenly didn't even want to think about the *additional* possibilities.

The final milestone—piling into the little host church that would be home for nine days. Girls in pews on the left. Guys in pews on the right. Leaders right down the center aisle. Cockroaches everywhere else. Juarez.

Right on time, 9:00 p.m., the little church filled, and we joined brothers and sisters for a worship service, having no idea that it would last three hours. We began watching the kids— sizzling kernels in a hot popcorn popper—to see who would explode first, hoping that it wouldn't be a grievous cultural boo-boo right off the bat. As the last song, or so I hoped, filled the air, Nate began pushing toward the back of the church. *Oh no,* I thought. *Don't burst, little guy. Dooooon't burst.*

I began *my* push toward the doors to block his escape, but he bolted past the doors and ran straight toward me. Bouncing up and down like a high-tension racquet ball, he began to blurt—not English, not Spanish, maybe not any language.

"Nate, sloooow down. Slow down." I put my hands on his shoulders, subduing the bounces inch by inch.

"Ms. L. Ms. L.! It's amazing! It's unbelievable! It's . . . well, it's . . . it's . . . "

"Nate, slow down," I whispered.

"Ms. L! Ms. L!" his voice was urgent. "We have stuff," he panted, wildly sweeping his arms back and forth, pointing at various things, "but these people have *STUFF!*" he declared while repeatedly poking his forefinger toward his heart.

"Wow." It was the only word I could mutter in the face of this profound revelation resonating in the heart of this little wild man. Here's Nate, already enlarging and challenging my own faith. What a start, and he had only just begun.

The days rolled on, and one by one various challenges touched and changed all of us. The kids witnessed true wealth in the midst of appalling poverty, hearty love in the midst of severe suffering, such sweet joy in the midst of deep deprivation. They did without hundreds of luxuries that they'd taken for granted for years. They stretched in ways they'd not thought possible.

We spent that trip working at an orphanage, trying to make living conditions a little easier to bear, but day by day, these students made friends, they touched hearts, they hugged orphans while they read to them and played with them and cried with them. Seventh graders still, but they were being transformed with wisdom and maturity born only in genuine giving and self-sacrifice.

Just after dinner on the eighth day, as a stunning sunset began to blaze in the west, it happened. Nate flew through the screen door, screaming, "Ms. L! Ms. L!" In giant leaps, he found me and grabbed my sleeve, jerking me toward the door with desperate tugs. My mind raced. *What now? What happened? Who's hurt?*

I broke into a run with him so he wouldn't dislocate my shoulder. Panic rose in me as his frenzy increased the farther we ran. Suddenly, Nate jerked me around the corner of a broken-down, wooden shed and stopped so abruptly that I nearly toppled over him and into five Mexican boys, causing a thick cloud of desert dust to envelop us.

"Do something, Ms. L.! Do something! Make them stop! Ms. L! Make them stop!" I had no idea what he saw that I didn't, but as the dust settled, my heart burst, almost choking me.

The boys, three tall teenagers and two younger ones, were throwing a tiny gray kitten around—up and down, back and forth—icy laughter erupting with each throw, tearing Nate's heart. Tearing my heart.

"Ms. L! Stop them! Make them stop!"

I didn't speak much Spanish, so I found my "use in case of emergency" teacher voice and broke into their circle, bellowing, "Stop!" I was sure the little gray kitten was dead, but I simply could not fail Nate. My heart pounded against my ribs. Hurt for the little kitten, hurt for Nate, and fearing for our safety, I had no clue what to do next; we were a long way from the safe little church.

Silence hung in the air, and a new hurt stung me, a hurt for these five boys. Anger, defiance, and emptiness filled their eyes. They were thin, ragged, and lost. Their own lives lifeless, inconsequential. Abused, malnourished, and unappreciated. *Not much different than the little gray kitten.*

Deep emotions pushed tears to my eyes. Nate's tears were already making tiny tracks down his dusty cheeks. Just then, he slipped in beside me. He stuck his hands into his pockets and pulled out the contents, letting the pockets hang inside out against his dirty jeans. Treasures spilled out—the kind of treasures that only a seventh-grade boy would love: A grimy rabbit's foot, two marbles, a rusty and odd-shaped nail, some crumpled bottle caps, a few pennies, a dollar and a dime, and a few little rocks. He placed all his treasures in one hand, and as he extended it to the group, he also extended his empty hand, palm up. As he moved his hands back and forth, his message transcended language: "I'll give you all of this if you will give me the kitten." Now my tears fell freely, too, and made little puffs as they hit the desert dirt.

Empty pockets. Nate was giving all he had in a desperate act of sacrifice to save the little kitten that still hung limply by his tail from a big boy's hand.

Minutes. Moments. Life-changing truth hung suspended in time. Nate had painted a perfect portrait of grace. I could see God the Father emptying His pockets and offering us forgiveness. I could see His tears and feel His love. Even though we were dead in sin, lifeless, empty, angry—just like these five boys—our heavenly Father emptied His pockets and gave us Jesus. Then Jesus emptied His pockets. He hung on that cross for us, just like the little kitten now hung, waiting for our answer to His offer.

The big boy finally dropped the kitten into Nate's empty hand, and Nate poured his treasures into the boy's rough hands. They turned and padded barefoot in one direction while Nate and I headed toward home. He cupped the tiny creature in his hands as if handling a priceless treasure and lifted it toward his face. He whispered to it. He stroked it. His tears bathed it. Secure in the little wild man's hands, the kitten opened its pale-blue eyes. It was alive!

We were alive! We stopped in our tracks and thanked God— thanked Him for the kitten's life, for our lives, for His love and empty pockets. We asked Him to go get the five boys and hold them like Nate held the little gray kitten. We loved on the tiny kitten with all we were and all we had, and then we silently shuffled home.

Our team nurse reluctantly gave Nate her one and only eyedropper, and he never closed his eyes that night as he fed and nursed and loved that kitten to strength. Distressed that he couldn't bring it with him into the States, he spent the entire next morning interviewing various families to see who would love the little one like he did. Finally satisfied, he handed the kitten to a pastor and his wife. Then he gave them the eyedropper and fully schooled them in how to feed his furry friend.

Now, years later, with every batch of laundry I do, I thank God for that little wild man and his perfect picture of grace that still stirs my soul and bends my knee—empty pockets forever redefined for me by Nate.

"EMPTY POCKETS" – FOR DEEPER THOUGHT . . .

1. How does Nate's story move your heart?

2. What have you thought about grace? How have your thoughts changed after watching Nate's sacrifice?

3. Have you ever emptied your pockets to save someone or something precious? What would emptying your pockets look like for you?

4. Are you wavering about the sacrifice Jesus made when He emptied Himself by dying on the cross to save you from your sins? Nate's sacrifice saved that kitten. Only Jesus's sacrifice can save a person from their sin. If you haven't surrendered your life to Jesus, what's holding you back?

5. If you believe in Jesus and have received Him as your Savior, to what degree have you emptied your pockets for Him and His work in the world? What changes do you feel you need to make, and how will you go about making them?

6. Philippians 2:7-11 tells us that Jesus "emptied Himself, taking the form of a bond-servant, and being made in the likeness of men . . . He humbled Himself by becoming obedient to the point of death, even death on a cross. For this reason also, God highly exalted Him, and bestowed on Him the name which is above every name, so that at the name of Jesus EVERY KNEE WILL BOW . . . and that every tongue will confess that Jesus Christ is Lord, to the glory of God the Father." How is your heart moved by these verses? What changes will you make as a result?

7. What youthful believers can you learn from? Who may be a "Nate" in your life?

Empty Pockets

How can it be that Almighty God sees me?
How can it be that Almighty God loves me?
That You would send Your one and only Son to
pay the price for my sin.
That you would write my name in the book of
life before time began.
(John 3:16; Romans 5:10)

Living Stones

Kilometer 29—the extreme outskirts of Juarez, Mexico, where humanity dares the desert to defeat it, and the desert dares humanity to defy it. Where hot winds snatch the sand and blast it against all impediments, pelting them into submission. Where the naked sun blisters backs and grants no grace even as it sets in washes of fiery yellows and golds laced with silver edges. Juarez, Mexico—where cockroaches reign and starving animals jerk tears from tender souls.

This is where I chose to spend a year's sabbatical from the Boulder middle school where I had been teaching English for three years. Over the previous ten years, the El Paso Youth with a Mission (YWAM) base had helped me bring scores of my middle school students to Kilometer 29 to build a school and a church. This particular sabbatical year I was teaching English at this little school, and I could hardly wait to help the incoming team build a "real" house for teachers.

I had grown to love the pastor at Kilometer 29 and the colony of people there. So instead of leading a team of students, this time I was helping Pastor Padilla host a new group of eight families. Our task for this group was to build a new house that Pastor Padilla hoped would shout, "Come, teachers! Live here. Teach here. We need you."

The old house held no appeal, whatsoever. I mean, even after three cases of caulk and shoveling out buckets of cockroaches, mold, and dead rodents, my tiny abode still hosted mice that played chase all night, running back and forth across me when I was desperate for sleep. But now, with this new group of workers just minutes away, all that was about to change. I watched the hands of my watch tick the seconds away with great excitement.

The roar of diesel trucks pulling trailers finally reached our ears. Shacks around the school emptied as families gathered at Pastor Padilla's house to help greet the newcomers. I scanned my notes. Many things had to be covered to help orient our visitors. Nothing would be familiar or easy for them.

Though excited, I had quiet doubts about how things would go, knowing the necessity of prayerful servant's hearts for effective missions work. This crucial work of prayer seemed to be in short supply during pre-trip meetings with the new group back in Colorado.

It only took a few minutes into orientation to confirm my suspicions. This group had experience with building wooden structures and had predetermined to do just that. They proudly proceeded to tell Pastor P. all the things they had planned to do—not *with* him—but *for* him.

This unassuming pastor, maybe five feet tall with black shaggy hair and dark weathered skin that folded into soft wrinkles when he smiled, listened and nodded as the group shared their expertise and told him exactly what they were going to do and how they were going to do it. Watching this humble servant of God patiently listen to this group outlining all their grand plans for Kilometer 29 warmed my heart. I loved working in this little man's neighborhood.

I laid my notes aside, and when they finished, Pastor P. smiled at them and glanced at me, black eyes twinkling, and then started shuffling toward the work site. Chattering like kids on a field trip, the group enthusiastically followed, certain that Pastor P. had agreed to all their impressive plans. Somewhat embarrassed, I began looking for the first opportunity to apologize to Pastor P., though I knew he'd say, "No Problemo."

We turned the last corner, and shock instantly silenced the group. Reality collided with pride like a wrecking ball smashing a wall. Towering stacks of cinder blocks. Sheets of metal roofing, rows of rebar, piles of rocky sand. Bulging cement bags laughed at us, layering everything in fine gray dust. *"Welcome to cinder-block building,"* they all seemed to taunt.

Egos bruised and communication a bit difficult with everyone speaking odd combinations of *Spanglish*, Pastor P. began showing the team what he knew needed to be done. He busied three people carrying buckets of water from an uncovered brick tank to the cement-mixing trays. The dead rodents, cockroaches, and other "floaties" in the water didn't faze Pastor P., but the threesome came back squeamishly pale, and they immediately lobbied for a different job—*any* job.

Four others followed this gentle man to a rocky "sand" pile, where they were to sift the mixture until only fine sand remained. Bound loosely together, splintered and cracked boards held together pieces of screen and other scraps of metal mesh. Two team members placed this contraption over a flat-tired, rusty wheelbarrow, and Pastor P. carefully placed a shovelful of stony sand on the screens. The mesh mess totally fell apart after two shakes.

The foursome then made crude repairs and tried again. Gingerly placing half a shovel of the gravely concoction on the sifter, they wisely decided against the shaking method. Instead, they used their hands to move the mixture back and forth and round and round, as if kneading dough. When only rocks remained, they carefully dumped them off to one side, focusing only on one thing—keeping the sifting contraption together.

The rock pile grew much faster than the good sand pile under the makeshift strainer; even so, two things became crystal clear. The water job was gruesome, and the next job of tackling the towers of blocks looming beside us was daunting. Thus, the sand job began to have strong appeal, no matter how tedious.

With Pastor P.'s tutelage, the rest of our group—the block bunch—began moving blocks one by one and strategically placing each one onto a concrete foundation at the edge of the property. After lifting, transporting, and placing a couple dozen blocks, now even the water job, with all its floaties, looked wonderful.

By noon, truth had hit each team member head-on. Any job in this sun-beaten land would drive people to the limit of their strengths and ruthlessly expose all weaknesses. Arrogance and selfishness stood no chance. Hearts and motives would be stripped naked, just like the wind-stripped land.

We paused for lunch, lost in individual thoughts, unable or unwilling to expend energy talking about what we faced or what we felt. The "waterers" nursed bloody blisters and open cuts on their hands; the "sanders" could not straighten their bent backs, and the "blockers" simply fell to the ground in various places begging to be spoon-fed. The childish, early-morning jealousy toward the "lunch" bunch, who could quit working thirty minutes early to prepare the food, had vanished. The trek to the school kitchen and back in the heat of the day sucked every ounce of strength out of already weary legs. Nobody looked forward to their turn serving lunch. Every group who had ever come to Kilometer 29 had been broken in order to learn how to serve. The first day here was always brutal but crucial in this breaking process.

Plodding back to the site, the lunch crew set out peanut butter-and-jelly sandwiches and oranges, then flopped down like rag dolls. Emotions whirled within me as I carefully sucked the juice from my orange sections, desperately trying to soothe my parched throat while cautiously avoiding the ragged cracks in my lips. Regret gnawed at my soul as I sensed the absolute discontent, even anger, in several members of this group. I struggled to stay positive about the coming days. Four hours of work had transformed the bravado of the morning into awkward silence. Aching bodies and bruised pride gave way to introspection. I had seen other groups hit the wall, but on previous trips with middle schoolers, I had watched them rebound quickly. This group, consisting of CEOs, entrepreneurs, scientists, engineers—leaders of all kinds— were not rebounding quite so quickly, however. I wondered how or even *if* they would rebound at all. I wondered which "chiefs" would become willing followers. I wondered when egos would concede and genuine teamwork begin.

One thing was certain—the desert would break them, and God would win.

As if sensing the groups' resistance, nature instantly responded with angry winds, swiping desert dirt from one place and violently driving it into Kilometer 29, biting skin, stinging eyes, clogging noses and sinuses, filling ears. Its accomplice, the noonday sun, continued glaring and sneering or burning and blistering all unprotected skin.

Pastor P. and I glanced at each other. The years of working together, on and off, had built a sweet kinship between us, an understanding that needed no words. We had seen God work in mysterious ways with people, and this group would be no exception. As Pastor P. put it, "We do our work, and God does His. No problemo. No problemo, Gloria a Dios."

Four brutal hours followed. Raw fingers stuck out of shredded gloves. Bloodshot eyes peeked through tightly squinted lids. Blisters broke, bled, and soaked dirty Band-Aids. Retorts flew. Nerves frayed. This group was already stretched far beyond their comfort levels. The harsh conditions had relentlessly assaulted their prowess and pride. Slowly, humility was finding its way into softened hearts and exhausted bodies.

Even the cinder blocks had refused to cooperate. That they were crude and rough was obvious, but no one could have guessed that they were different lengths until the bottom row was completed. The teams had worked from the corners in, and not one row met in the center. All four sides had spaces of varying lengths. The group bit their chapped lips, not daring to vocalize their anger and discouragement.

"No problemo! No problemo!" Pastor P. encouraged, patting team members on the back, coaxing them toward the cafeteria. This sweet shepherd knew they needed food and rest, for this man's kind heart beat for the sheep—not for the structure they were building.

Conversation at dinner consisted of short, often curt quips, and nobody needed reminding of the curfew hour. Lights blinked off quickly.

I woke before the roosters and headed to the work site, asking the Lord about the "no problemo" spaces that had to be fixed somehow. Several minutes later, Ed, a well-known CEO of a very successful business, joined me.

Oh, Lord, thank You, I prayed silently.

We chatted awhile, pitching ideas and possibilities back and forth until finally settling on two things: One, we wouldn't work toward the middle but instead from one corner, staggering the weak spots throughout each wall, making sure that no two spaces were too close together; and two, someone would attempt to cut blocks to custom fit all these holes. Of course, there were no electric saws even close to Kilometer 29, so how we would do this "cutting" was quite mysterious. But we high fived each other and headed back for breakfast, energized by the "staggered block" plan, though a little suspicious about the "custom-fit" plan.

Yay, God! Thank You, I prayed, silently praising Him for Ed, because Pastor P. and I now had a true partner—a gifted man and problem-solver—working *with* us, certainly a step in the right direction.

Days two and three followed much the same course, and spacing the holes became easier and almost fun—like putting together a jigsaw puzzle. Laughter even found its way into the work. A second positive step. However, the increasing number of spaces began begging for attention. Ed explained what needed to be done, and no one jumped up to volunteer, he looked at me, shrugged his shoulders, and began measuring the spaces.

"No problemo," I chirped and began searching for a way to fill the spaces.

Ed handed me a list of lengths for thirteen filler blocks, and I went to work with typical Juarez tools—an odd piece of metal that just barely resembled a chisel and a splintered hammer held together by various tapes, strings, and nails. After multiple failures and a growing pile of useless, broken blocks, I moved my work station into the pile of sand.

Hurrying had proved fruitless. Obviously, these blocks needed tender loving care if they were ever going to break where they were supposed to break. So, I plopped a block in the sand and began scoring it all the way around with hundreds of gentle, tiny hammer taps on the chisel. They held together much better as the soft sand cushioned the scoring process.

It was painstakingly slow and meticulous work. Eventually, I carefully placed the chisel on the top edge where the block had been scored, tapped on one side, then on the other top edge. I repeated this until small cracks began working their way down the scores on both sides. After six or seven taps on both sides, the block fell into two smooth-edged pieces. "Yes!" I hollered. All eyes turned my way, and everyone clapped. "Who needs one 4-and-3/8-inch filler block?" I yelled, thrilled as the cutting process took shape.

Ed ran over to grab it. High tens this time. God was indeed blessing the time we took seeking Him before the day began. Others began clambering, "Mine next! 2 and 3/4!"

I laid another block in the sand to begin the slow process once again. *Geeze,* I thought. *Almost an hour of work for one usable block. I'll never finish.* Immediately the Lord made His presence palpable.

"Living stones, Kathy. Living stones being built into a spiritual household. I must work slowly and steadily and ever so gently as My sheep are fragile and shatter quite easily. I'm in no hurry. One useable child is priceless in My hands."

I exhaled slowly and sank my knees deeper into the sand, bowing before my incredible Lord who calls us by name, who hears us, and who speaks to us. He was speaking now about this precious process explained in 1 Peter 2:4–5. I closed my eyes and breathed Him in, overflowing with love and worship for Jesus, the Cornerstone who was rejected by men but precious in the sight of God, the Cornerstone who is working with *us,* His living stones, building us up into a holy priesthood, tapping us, scoring us, changing us, custom-fitting us for His pleasure, for His service.

Oh, my Lord. Thank You. Have Your Way. Do Your work here today, with each of us.

I snuggled another block into the sand and began tapping and scoring. With each block, I prayed for one team member, lifting them up to the Lord, asking Him to tap and score them for His service, for His pleasure. I caught up quickly, the work no longer painstakingly slow, but beautiful and sweet.

Pastor P. also consistently interceded for each team member as they worked—still perfunctory and somewhat-forced labor, not yet a labor of heart or spirit for all; but we were inching forward, and we had never seen God fail. He would not fail this group either—His living stones.

Day four brought fast progress on the structure. Row by row, the house grew taller while each brick grew heavier. It soon took two people to hoist these crude cinder blocks to the next height. As the hours sapped strength and will, it soon took three people to muscle the blocks up. Teamwork was emerging, like a tight bud slowly unfolding, with each layer so beautiful and satisfying, moving toward fullness.

Over the years and with every group, we'd gather after dinner for a time of praise and worship and prayer. That, too, was forced and fairly ineffective the first three days. I told Pastor P. I didn't think I'd do it the fourth evening. Discouragement dogged me as the stubbornness of some of the "stones" seemed unbreakable. But he just grinned, grabbed his guitar, and headed to the dorm rooms, inspiring me to follow. "No problemo, Kat, no problemo. Let's do it." Oh, how I loved this dear brother. Rivers of living water poured out of him as naturally as the sun poured out light and heat on Kilometer 29.

This dear man's infectious faith and unencumbered authentic worship began melting the team. One by one, as the group recognized choruses sung in Spanish, they joined in with heartfelt English. There were smiles and laughter, even raised hands here and there—small surrenders to the great Potter who takes the clay and reworks it, forming His design;

to the Cornerstone who taps and scores and breaks His living stones to "custom fit" His Kingdom purposes.

Pastor Padilla's guitar jumped to life with one of my favorite choruses. "He is the King of Kings. He is the Lord of Lords. His name is Jesus, Jesus, Jesus, ooooooooooooh He is the King." Each time Pastor P. held the "oh" longer and longer till we all burst out laughing. All tension finally broke. Façades fell. We sang simply as brothers and sisters in Christ. Just servants at Kilometer 29, building a block house to bring God glory and helping this dear pastor reach the lost of this barren, burnt place.

I woke with great expectancy on day five. God inhabits the praises of His people, and He had certainly touched hearts through Pastor P.'s worship. Oh, how it showed. The self-appointed chiefs had pretty much disappeared. One jumped in to help the "floaties" bunch get the buckets of water to the cement-mixing place. Two others combined their engineering skills and quite ingeniously reinforced the sifting screen and began wearing out their gloves and backs. Another showed his wife how to cement a brick into place as he lifted it for her. Soon the older kids were helping each other lift, place, and cement blocks, too. No longer were they just being ordered here and there as gofers.

Everyone's interest levels soared! The worksite hummed with teamwork and cohesiveness. When humility reigns, it gives birth to real service where work done for the Lord is not just personal satisfaction. Even the young ones had a perfect place in the process. What's better than having a big sandbox to play in? We found various containers for them to transport the sifted sand to the mixing area. Some even found that stirring the sand into the cement and water was quite entertaining. One precocious sixth-grader dropped into the sand with me and asked if I could show him how to cut the "special" blocks.

Spontaneous laughter mixed with "Good job" and "Way to go" and "Yep! That's it!" created a sweet worship of its own to the Lord who had led this group to this very moment at Kilometer 29. As spirit and heart took control, energy multiplied. They took Pastor P.'s "No problemo" as their team motto. Even the lunch bunch hustled back and forth from the kitchen with new vim and vigor, and we all stayed an hour longer to put the finishing touches on the last level.

After dinner, the men gathered with Pastor P. and, putting all their skills together, developed an ingenious way of getting the roof on. They included Pastor P. in every thought and idea and decision—the total opposite of that first day. Humility certainly creates cohesiveness.

Pastor Padilla and I hadn't even planned on getting the roof done after watching the pace of the first few days. However, as God broke this group and filled them with the energy of the Holy Spirit, they too fell in love with Pastor P. In response to his heart and humility, they committed themselves totally to finishing this new house for him, and now, *with* him.

Worship that fifth evening was the kind that touches heaven and makes God smile. Egos had disappeared and hearts had surrendered. Spontaneous prayers erupted following worship. Prayers for the people of Kilometer 29, for Mexico, for Pastor P., for teachers and students, for each other, for God to be glorified in their last day, and—yes—prayers for the roof to get done. Way past curfew, we turned the lights out, full of the satisfaction of humble service. There's nothing quite like it.

The sixth day began almost as a race. The men focused on the roof while the rest of us formed four teams, each armed with buckets of cement and trowels. We were to fill all the cracks and make things smooth—as much as that was possible with these rough, ragged blocks.

Well past lunchtime, Pastor P. and I snuck away and headed to the kitchen. Even when we returned with food and drinks, the work hummed along. One by one, we tossed sandwiches and water bottles to workers when they could take a few minutes.

God's transforming work was clearly displayed—taking individuals and turning them into a team with a higher goal than self and lunch. This roofed house for Pastor P.'s new teachers and the people of Kilometer 29 took precedence over all else.

Washes of pink and gold began brushing the desert sky, gently announcing day's end. Whoops and hollers and hallelujahs greeted the sunset as each group finished, then hurried to help another group until the job was done.

No one *led* worship that last evening. We simply worshiped in spontaneously humble communion with our Creator. Then, tired to the bone but filled to the brim with spirit, we began packing what wasn't needed and cleaning what could be cleaned in preparation for the team's departure the next morning.

At the break of dawn, Pastor Padilla's praise rang through the neighborhood as he walked to the church, playing his guitar and worshiping the Lord with the great gusto that defined this little man and everything he did. People piled into the church, and Pastor P. preached with power. This neighborhood of believers, so poor in things of this world yet so rich in the Spirit, drew us up into mighty worship and thanksgiving.

With the last amen, we helped the team finish packing, and we all gathered in the new block house. We held hands, and I opened in prayer. Stunning is the only word that fits what happened next. One of the men left the circle and went straight to Pastor Padilla, tears running down His face, confessing his pride and ego and asking for forgiveness. He was followed by another, then another. Some team members went to other team members. A few parents went to kids and other parents. Several kids went to parents.

Right here in this barren land, in this house of rough, ragged cinder blocks, Peter's words came full circle. This team, God's living stones, had been built up into a spiritual house and were now freely offering up sweet spiritual sacrifices to Jesus, the precious Cornerstone. Confession. Repentance. Humility of heart.

They arrived at Kilometer 29 as one group but left as quite another. The Lord's chiseling and scoring and breaking was successful again, something only He can do, something He loves to do for His living stones.

"LIVING STONES" – FOR DEEPER THOUGHT . . .

1. Have you been in a situation where you've thought your way was the best way and perhaps the only way, but where you didn't actually get your way? How did that work out?

2. Proverbs 27:17 says, "Iron sharpens iron, So one man sharpens another." As you think about the situation in question one, how would this verse change your behavior and/ or thinking?

3. When you are stretched to your limit and think you cannot go on, what do you do?

4. "No test or temptation that comes your way is beyond the course of what others have had to face. All you need to remember is that God will never let you down; he'll never let you be pushed past your limit; he'll always be there to help you come through it" (1 Corinthians 10:13 MSG). How does this Scripture change your thinking, and what will you do differently the next time you are in a tough circumstance?

5. "And coming to Him as to a living stone which has been rejected by men, but is choice and precious in the sight of God, you also, as living stones, are being built up as a spiritual house for a holy priesthood, to offer up spiritual sacrifices acceptable to God through Jesus Christ" (1 Peter 2:4–5). Knowing that Jesus, the living Cornerstone (Ephesians 2:20), is building us in the midst of our tests and trials, how does this encourage you?

6. How have these truths changed your thinking about difficult circumstances?

7. How will your responses to tough situations change in light of these truths?

Living Stones

Take me, my Lord, and break me
again if You need to.
Mold me, Oh Lord, please make me
a reflection of You.
Lord, here I'll stay with You,
please have Your way.
I surrender to You as soft clay.
(Romans 9:21; Isaiah 64:8)

The Right Thing

For some wild reason, the Lord plopped me into a family when I returned to the States from missionary time overseas. Psalm 68 says that He sets the lonely in families, and though *I* wasn't lonely, He *did* set me in this young family that had a huge vacant spot. Dad wasn't in the home, and pain wracked the four of them in various ways. Mary, my sweet friend and mother to Gail, Jake, and Mark, welcomed me in as one of the family, and for twelve years we lived and moved and had our being as a unit of five. Sharing meals, tears, trials, and growing pains, but also sharing a faith that made it all work. Our mission trips, mostly into Juarez, Mexico, etched priceless memories on our hearts. Working and ministering together in such horrible conditions deepened our relationships like unique colors in a tightly knit sweater. I had the honor of teaching the kids, first in a private Christian school, and then in a home school group that included several other children outside the family. The years went by too quickly.

When Gail turned sixteen, she signed up for the greatest trip of her young life. The lepers in India had tugged at her heart, and she would be spending three months with them. That precocious third-grader had turned into an amazing young woman with God's heart for lepers. Several dear friends gathered for her send-off. I played the guitar and sang a song that God had given me for Gail, and we all laid hands on her and prayed our hearts out.

It was so sweet and satisfying to watch this young woman head into missionary work overseas because she wanted her faith stretched—Gail so wanted to be used by God. I brimmed with pride at who she was in Christ, and I put my concern into one constant prayer: *India. Lepers. Oh, Lord, go before her.*

Two days after this wonderful send-off, things exploded. I wasn't exactly kicked out, but I had to leave. Each year, as Mark—the youngest child in the family—grew older and bigger, his abusive tendencies grew as well. When he attacked his mother one day, I called 911 to protect her. She was furious.

She was no match for her angry young teenager, but as things usually go with family members, the outsider is the problem. Mary defended Mark, and a twelve-year friendship ended in an unraveled relationship and broken hearts. I moved out, barely breathing. The loss suffocated me throughout the entire summer and well beyond.

In this very fragile state, the day arrived for Gail's welcome-home party. I told the Lord *again*, "I can't do this." In a thousand ways, I kept telling Him, "I can't go back there. It's just too painful." In my sorrow, though, one thought persistently pushed through the pain. *It's the right thing to do.* "Oh, God, I *know* it's the right thing to do . . . for You, and . . . for Gail, but I can't do it," I repeated again and again but to no avail. I was tenderly pressed into submission by the gentle Good Shepherd, so I headed east to Mary's house, reminding Him minute by minute that, "I still can't do this."

My only solace was that I would see all the dear friends again who helped send Gail off. I took four hits on my inhaler to ease the wheezing; took a long, slow, deep breath to calm my trembling; and knocked on the door. *Odd. For twelve years this was home. Now I'm knocking.* Waves of fear and hurt pounded my heart.

When Mary opened the door, I managed to squeak out a soft "Hi," before rushing past her to the upstairs bathroom, fighting emotions that threatened to pull me into deep water. My inhaler wasn't designed to help this kind of suffocation. *Oh, Lord. I'm here . . . trying to do the right thing. Please! Help!* I turned the faucet on to hide my sobs and waited. *Please, Lord. Breathe your breath into me.* I continued to wait. I closed my eyes and imagined Him breathing life into me. Breathing courage and strength into me. I concentrated on taking slow, long, deep breaths. Breathing in the Holy Spirit.

Thank you, Lord. Thank you. Thank You.

I steadied myself, wiped my tears, and started down the stairs. *Lord, WE can do this.* It was a fragile faith, but it *was* faith.

The room was packed, but there wasn't one familiar face in the whole group—a fairly boisterous group, oddly dressed. The women were my age but dressed more like college girls, low-cut blouses and short, short skirts. Not one person with whom we'd done so many mission trips was there. *Lord, I am so out of place here. Lord, I can't d . . . I . . . Lord, We can do this,* I told myself again and headed toward Gail, who had just begun opening her picture albums.

Those blue eyes, filled with the unique joy that humble service brings, welcomed me along with a giant, genuine hug. In an instant, Gail and I reconnected through missions, our common passion. She began sharing the struggles she overcame, how she planned to go back, and how she already missed those she came to love so deeply.

Easy. Free. We had spanned the chasm between us with the love that had been strong for years. Teacher. Substitute mom, at times. Friend.

One lady joined us, but the rest—totally disinterested in Gail's pictures and the stories of her heart—sat around telling jokes, talking about the houses or cars they'd just bought and other out-of-place things. I couldn't help but wonder why they had come. I couldn't help but wonder why Mary had traded the group that sent Gail off for this new group. Such a drastic difference.

"Okay, ladies. Please quiet down so Gail can share," Mary interrupted. Gail squeezed my hand, silently communicating, "I'm so glad you're here." Somehow it felt as if we were comrades against an enemy, and totally outnumbered. *Really weird.*

"So, Gail, tell us," a woman with layer upon layer of makeup began. "You didn't actually *touch* any lepers, did you?"

"Well, of course. They ar . . ."

"Oh! Leprosy's contagious. Maybe you shou . . . maybe we should wash our h—"

"No, here is how leprosy works," Gail butted in, somewhat irritated. She shared in measured words what she'd learned about leprosy and how precious these people were to her and to God. Some listened, but most of the group looked totally bored.

"And here is where we had to get water," Gail explained as she showed a picture with a pipe just above ground spewing out brown liquid.

"Ew! I just couldn't stand that. I wouldn't go there if someone paid me. I mean, why go? It doesn't change anything," another woman spouted.

"People go to these countries because the Lord says to go. He tells us to care for the sick and poor. That's why Gail went,"

I blurted out, more than somewhat irritated. "Gail, go ahead. Tell us about the water."

As she continued, my mind raced, trying to figure out what was really going on. *Why had these people even come? They had zero interest in missions or Gail.* Gail and I were *both* out of place! I was so thankful that the Lord had brought me, for *her* sake.

The next picture showed where Gail lived while in India. The comments really flew then.

"Gail, didn't you take any make-up? You look so pale."

"I would never live in a place like that! Look how filthy it is."

"Yeah, me neither!"

"Well, that's enough. I see no reason to take trips like this. What a waste of time."

Mary just sat there while these people badgered her daughter. Anger rose in me, pushing past my pain. I was just about to erupt when the doorbell rang and another woman sheepishly stepped into the room. I motioned her to the empty seat next to me, already feeling sorry for her to be in this strange group.

"Hi, I'm Diane. Sorry I'm late."

No one even acknowledged her presence. She might as well have been invisible.

Gail shared one more picture and stopped. Winking at me, she whispered, "You and I will do this together at another time, okay? These guys just don't get it."

"You bet," I agreed.

I hung around for another ten minutes or so. Mary never said a word to me and sat off to the side while the rest, totally self-absorbed, chatted about trivial things.

I sensed something was up with Diane, so I drew her in, as best as I could. Finally, I hugged Gail good-bye, excused myself, and invited Diane to come with me to check on my kitty. Barnabas was still at Mary's because I couldn't take him with me to my present home. I still had the code to the garage, where Mary kept him, and would sneak minutes with him several times a week when no one was home. I missed him terribly.

Diane immediately picked him up and cuddled him. Tears trickled down her face. "His silver coat is so beautiful and so soft. Is he a Seal Point?" she asked.

"I have no clue. I just know he's the best cat I've ever had. He's my best friend."

She nodded, and as her tears increased, Barnabas snuggled into her tightly, doing his best to tend her heart with his rhythmic purring.

"There is an evangelist named Barnabas in the Bible. His name means encourager," I explained, watching Barney's front paws making muffins on her arm.

"Yeah, that's the perfect name."

We both kissed the little guy good-bye, and I walked Diane to her truck. She sank into the driver's seat but didn't turn toward the wheel, as if she was waiting for something.

"Diane, I don't know you, but something awfully heavy is weighing on your heart. I'll listen," I encouraged.

Tears began again. "Do you know why I was late?" she asked, looking up at me with light-brown eyes drowning in anguish. "I was at the library searching for names so I can rename myself."

Having no clue how to respond, I nodded and waited for her to continue.

"My husband committed suicide. I don't want my name."

"Oh, Diane, I'm so sorry," I said and laid my hand on her shoulder.

"I came home. Looked into my living room window. Rick was hanging there."

Oh, my Lord. Please minister to this dear woman! I prayed silently.

"So, I must do something. I have to change something. I thought a new name might give me a new beginning," she blurted, her head almost dropping into her lap. "I have to find hope somehow."

I quickly squatted down and put my hands on both of her shoulders. She slumped forward, her head resting on my shoulder. "Diane," I whispered, "may I pray for you?" She weakly gave one little nod. "Oh, Lord," I began and just poured my heart out, hoping it was His heart for Diane, that it would hit the mark as only the Comforter can do. "Diane," I continued, "you are precious. You are lovely. You are cherished. You are . . ." I continued as if God was personally "renaming" her by telling her how He felt about her.

Her sobbing stopped. She sat straight up. A glimmer of hope shone in her eyes. "How did you know the names that I had just written down at the library?" she asked, pulling a carefully folded piece of paper out of her back pocket. As she unfolded it, I saw Precious. Cherished. Lovely. Hope, Faith, and a few names I couldn't quite make out.

"I didn't know what you wrote, Diane, but God did. God saw the names you chose, the names you needed to help you find a reason to live."

"Do you know I prayed when I left the library? I told God I was going to kill myself if He didn't intervene. I told Him if He didn't send someone to me, I was going right home after this party to kill myself. Everything is ready at home to do what my husband did."

"Well, God heard you. God loves you, Diane, and those names are who you are to Him. He *did* bring me because I was not going to come here today. This is the last place I wanted to be."

"Oh, Kathy, He did answer, didn't He? He wants me to live!"

"Absolutely! He arranged this exact moment for you. This is a direct answer to your prayer," I affirmed. "And, Diane, He will give you everything you need to recover and live fully."

We hugged and prayed and praised God.

"So, what name do you think you'll choose?"

"I choose Diane, and I'll remember that He sees me as precious, lovely, and cherished, and that gives me hope. I'll never forget how I prayed and He answered—how He stopped my suicide plan." We hugged again, humbled and in awe of our amazing God. Diane drove away a new woman. A woman touched by the Almighty in her deadly desperation. And I sat in my car for quite some time, stunned by what God had just done. How badly I wanted to stay home and not do this hard thing. The words of Psalm 37 ran through my mind: "Oh, Lord, thank you for ordering my steps today. Thank you for getting me here today." The hard thing to do is often the right thing to do. This hard thing for me to do was right because God had more on His heart than I knew at the time. Oh, how sweet that He allowed me to share in His plans for them. How gracious that He ordered my steps that day to do the *right* thing.

To do *His* thing.

"THE RIGHT THING" –
FOR DEEPER THOUGHT . . .

1. When did you do something that you dreaded doing? How did it work out?

2. Have there been times when someone called you or visited or sent a card at just the right time, when you needed it the most? Record those times and the results. How could you do something similar for someone?

3. Is there anything right now that you know you should do but haven't done yet? What is holding you back?

4. When a name or situation comes to mind that you could encourage someone, how do you respond? Do you gloss over it and get on with whatever you were doing? Do you take action? In what other ways could you respond?

5. You truly could be the answer to someone's prayer. How does this change your thinking?

6. Isaiah has an amazing encounter with God in Isaiah 6, and he eventually hears the voice of the Lord saying, "Whom shall I send, and who will go for Us?" Instantly, Isaiah responds, "Here am I. Send me!" (Isaiah 6:8). How might your life change if you made yourself available to be sent?

7. Jesus meets a desperate woman in John chapter 8. The religious leaders tell Him she was caught in adultery and should be stoned. Trying to trap Him, they asked, "What then do You say?" He answers, "He who is without sin among you, let him be the first to throw a stone at her." They left, one by one, and Jesus told the woman, "I do not condemn you, either. Go. From now on sin no more" (John 6:5-11). How might the Lord want to use you to build up someone who needs help? Who in your circle could use some support or encouragement? List the ways you could come to their aid.

8. "The steps of a man are established by the LORD, and He delights in his way" (Psalm 37:23). How might your days change if you asked the Lord to establish your steps? How might this make more room in your life to be sent and used by the Lord?

The Right Thing

For You know the plans that You have for me,
plans for a future and a hope.
You promise to make the rough places smooth
and make the crooked way straight.
(Jeremiah 29:11)

Beyond Words

We left Louisville at 4:00 a.m. with eighteen of my seventh-grade students, two leaders, and two YWAM staffers. Youth with a Mission (YWAM) specializes in worldwide, short-term mission trips, and my plan each school year was a nine-day YWAM mission trip into Juarez, Mexico, with my middle school students.

Now, there probably isn't any real magic in the number *nine*, and it certainly doesn't have the significance of biblical numbers like one, three, seven, or even eight, but after several of these trips, I've discovered nine is the perfect number. Longer and the kids wouldn't make it in the brutal heat and horrible conditions. Shorter and they wouldn't be softened enough to want God to reshape their lives.

Now, middle schoolers are—well, they are—middle schoolers. What else need be said? At their best, they are small bundles of unrefined, emotional energy that need peeled off the wall several times a day. But at 4:00 a.m., going on a road trip together to Mexico? It's like traveling with tightly packed fireworks, ready to explode at any moment. The trip takes about nineteen hours—if all goes smoothly. Parents like the security of a time line, so we tell them nineteen hours. But seriously, "If all goes smoothly?" Does a mission trip like that even exist?

The great mystery—the greatest fun each year—is wondering just which day the Lord will choose to interrupt our trip itinerary. What we do know, however, is that His appearance usually coincides quite closely with breakdowns of various types. The tired old bus that we take holds roughly forty-five people, and if necessary, other groups join us so that we can pack it full each trip. The narrow seats are like hard park benches. The air conditioning hasn't worked for years. The toilet works about half the time, and cruising speed uphill is around 40 mph—almost 55 miles per hour downhill, if we're lucky.

So, to fill our bus, our first stop was at a huge church in south Denver where we picked up seventeen high-school students and two more leaders. The second the bus stopped, our kids squirted out to help the "big" kids load their stuff, and sparks flew. Their unbridled enthusiasm stabbed the cocky, stoic demeanor of the Denver group like picks into ice. Fragments went everywhere. Angry words. Rude teasing. Mocking. Pushing. Shoving.

We charged into the centers of the worst scuffles like referees trying to separate overcharged athletes: totally outnumbered, totally unheeded. I quickly stuck two fingers to my lips and let out a whistle that pierced everyone's ears. Instantly, heads jerked around. As I searched for the right words and for the right heart from which to speak those words, several thoughts bounced around in my head. *An hour into the trip, and we have this total emotional breakdown. Lord, what do I say? What do we do with this?*

I searched their eyes, hoping mine were sending a clear message, though I wasn't even sure what that message was yet. When they dialed in, I began. "We are a *team*. We are heading to Juarez to *serve*. This behavior doesn't fit team or service. Those who already have a seat, go sit. Those who need to finish loading, finish. The bus leaves in five minutes."

We leaders huddled together, bowed our heads, and asked for God's wisdom and direction for this "team" of students. It was certainly the most combustible group we had ever taken to Juarez, and we really didn't know what to do to *undo* what had just happened. Words—cutting and hurtful. Attitudes—selfish and hateful. Hearts—arrogant and cold. One by one, the older kids boarded and sat. The atmosphere in the bus? Bitter cold.

Oh, Lord, we need You to intervene.

Mike, our driver, turned the key and we headed south. Another hour passed, and the bus suddenly bucked and burped and died. Just like that. This was the earliest bus breakdown on record. Obviously, God had a lot of work to do with this bunch. It was clear that He wanted to mold this group of rivals into a team and that He wanted to do it now. If this group was going to bless the orphans, the broken, and the hopeless of Juarez, they needed heart surgery over the next eighteen hours or so.

While Mike "worked" on the bus, we formed a large circle, held hands, and asked the Lord to come work amongst us. We waited silently to see what He wanted to do. A few kids found the boldness to pray—a few confessed their bad attitudes, and some asked for forgiveness. Their prayers were sweet fragrances lifted to the heavens, blessing God's heart and ours, the first fruits of the Spirit's work among us.

Just as the sun's first glimmers touched the eastern horizon, we broke the circle so the kids could move to each other and begin friendships. Many stood resolute and hard, but at least a deep work had begun. Our hearts swelled with the possibilities. What would the end of our trip look like when in just two hours we had experienced both a meltdown and a breakdown?

With the apologies completed, we made only one demand.

"We're a *team,* and our goal is to *serve.* It starts now. Older team members, find a younger team member to sit with. Spend the next hours getting to know each other. During our next stop, find a way to serve each other. Also, you will introduce each other and share at least two things that you learned about your teammate."

Aside from grumblings here and there, this pairing took just a few minutes. We formed another circle, ages interwoven this time. We held hands again and watched golden shafts of light rise and set the sky on fire. We prayed together for God to set our hearts on fire. Towers of selfishness and arrogance began weakening. Praises rose, and humility tiptoed in as God's light filled the sky—and us.

As our "amen" chorus ascended, the bus chugged to life! A miracle to be sure! I mean, Mike was a wonderful guy, but he knew absolutely nothing about engines. We had been on enough trips together to know that God was big on bus breakdowns. They were His "time-outs" to work in hearts. Mike and I also knew that God always started the bus when *He* was ready. I shot him a quick look, and he just grinned, shrugged his shoulders, and pointed to the heavens. He was the first to admit that all he did when he lifted the hood was pray. Chuckling, I turned toward the slowly developing team and hollered, "The bus leaves in five minutes."

My mind drifted to the sweet expectancy of Psalm 5. In the morning, God hears us; we lay our requests before Him and wait with expectation for Him to act. And, He *always* does.

Way behind schedule now, we put aside our itinerary to focus only on the Lord's plan for this group of youngsters and on our own hearts to cooperate with Him and His plan. The conversations that buzzed throughout the bus thrilled us. Kids were learning about each other so that they could begin loving each other. Only then would they be able to love the people and culture of those we would serve.

We still had a long way to go to become effective servants in the desert, where the blinding sun and crushing heat exposed every weakness and sin. But God had begun the work only He could do, and we knew that He would finish what He had for this group by day nine.

As a staff, we geared up for our first pit stop, knowing it could easily be the next breakdown. All kinds of things happen when thirty-five youngsters hit the snacks and bathrooms at the same time, all trying to do what needs done in fifteen minutes—always the goal of pit stops but seldom the reality.

Three of us posted ourselves as lookouts around the front of the building to coax "strays" to go straight to the bus. Two of us pounded on bathroom doors trying to hurry the process along, and two more supervised the snack attack. One stood by the bus counting heads and urging students to board quickly. It was a lot like herding cats—frenetic and fun.

Those who hit the goal and boarded in fifteen minutes got a secret prize that included the first choice of seats and pointed toward privileges once we got to Juarez. Obviously, the efficiency of the next pit stop skyrocketed, and teamwork improved dramatically as highly motivated seventh-graders, who will do almost anything for rewards, pulled and pushed and prodded their less-motivated, more "mature" teammates to meet the time limit.

With the head count right, Mike hit the key, and we headed south. Kids shared and traded snacks, interacted and laughed, chattering a mile a minute. As the hum of the bus quieted, teammates began sharing things they had learned about each other while the rest listened. The ice had thawed. The atmosphere? Warm, comfortable.

At each pit stop, everyone found a new teammate as we continued south. Focusing more and more on each other and less on self, we learned new things and moved forward. Amazing. Actually, it was breathtaking to watch as the Lord transformed individuals into a team and then moved each one toward servanthood.

Three hours later than expected, we finally reached Juarez, where these kids would be stretched to their breaking points, where they would see and experience things that would shock them, where they would interact with their Lord in ways they never imagined. What a great privilege it was to do this with them.

Pastor Gomez scurried out to greet us and hustled us to the classrooms that were to be our bedrooms for the next nine days. Throwing sleeping bags down on concrete floors, we grabbed maybe four hours of sleep before ministry began. No one needed to be coaxed to sleep.

Roosters rule as the official alarm clock in Juarez, and they strongly believe that their job does not have to wait for sunrise. No one can sleep through the cacophony, so 5:00 a.m. was up-n-at-em time, much to the dismay of our kids. The first shock.

The next shock followed breakfast. Back in the bus, we drove about twenty-five miles to a place called Agua Viva, Living Water, a last-chance rehab center for addicts of all kinds. The squeals of the kids who were wide awake quickly jerked the sleepers into alertness. Even though we spent time telling our teams about the service we would give, when *their* reality hit *desert* reality, shock was inevitable.

Mike geared down to safely make the sharp turn into the compound, giving the team a firsthand look at unbelievable squalor and suffering. Exclamations erupted from every direction.

"Hey! Look at all the pens. What kind of animals do they keep here?"

"Whatever they are, I feel sorry for them. There's no water or food!"

"How could anything live out here?"

"How can we possibly be of any help here?"

Then, as Mike carefully inched the bus to its spot, the realities collided. "Ohhh, man! Those aren't animals in there. They're people!"

Gasps of horror filled the bus just as Pastor Raul stepped onboard. I admired this amazing man of God. We had worked together before, and I had never met anyone so selfless. I hugged him and turned to our kids.

"It's okay, you guys. I know it's hard to see men living like this, but they're here for a special reason and so are we. We're going to help them build dorm rooms." I nodded for Raul to take over.

"Hi. I'm Pastor Raul, and we are thrilled to have you here. We've been praying that God would bring us help, and He has answered us. He has brought you. The work you do here will give these men *real* rooms. We are even believing God for beds!" he declared and laughed.

At ease now, the kids began noticing the men surrounding the bus, waving, smiling, speaking as much English as they knew to welcome us, some praising God with tears and uplifted hands. Just like that, our kids couldn't get off the bus fast enough. They started shaking hands, speaking what Spanish they knew, hugging, making friends, touching hearts. And best of all? The older kids helped the timid kids like big brothers and big sisters do. The dividing walls had vanished. God had done what He alone could do on a twenty-two-hour bus ride. This *team* was free to serve now.

Oh, how can I describe our seven days at Agua Viva? How can I explain the hearts of the men there? Desperate, helpless, and once-hopeless men, coming to Agua Viva for their last chance to break the chains that bound them—throwing themselves on the love of Jesus alone. Humble men on their faces before God, hungering and thirsting for Him.

There was no doctor there, no therapist, no counselor, no medicine, no twelve-step program. Sometimes there was no food. On drastic days, there was no water when the truck that filled the tank broke down. But God was there. *The* Counselor, the Holy Spirit, lived there and moved there, setting men free.

The corner pen—the only pen that hadn't emptied? That was the prayer closet. Every second of every day there were three "free" men in that pen interceding for the rest, begging the Spirit to set the captives free. Fasting and taking twelve-hour shifts, three men shut themselves in to seek God. When they came out, the next three went in. They urgently, constantly covered Agua Viva in prayer—prayer that God heard; prayer that God acted upon.

While the men gave the kids a grand tour, Raul helped the leaders set up for the lunch we brought with us. The lunch "bell" was a boisterous round of "Our God is an Awesome God." The men knew the signal, and as they gathered the kids and joined us, we grabbed hands and filled the heavens with praise, proclaiming that our God is awesome over and over and over. Our voices caught up, perhaps, with the heavenly choir around the throne of grace. This was real, rich worship in this desperate barren corner of the earth, way beyond just words—deep calling to deep.

Way beyond what the kids had ever experienced, this was worship that nearly touched the holy. Perhaps like what Isaiah spoke of when He saw the Lord high and lifted up on a throne,

His robe filling the temple, the angels crying, "Holy, Holy, Holy is the Lord." The kind of worship that undoes the worshiper, where one needs to just fall facedown in His presence in silent awe.

As His presence hovered over us, we broke bread together, the fellowship so sweet, formed strong bonds. These naïve youngsters and these broken men laughed and shared and served one another. Once again, simply amazing.

Before we left, we formed eight groups, with the men as leaders. They showed us what we would be doing and how we would do it. Concerned for our safety, they cautioned us about the things that might be dangerous. They showed us what had been done by other groups and announced that we would help them finish their cinder-block dorms so that the team coming in two weeks could put the windows in and the roof on. We clapped and cheered at the word "finish." We shared hugs and headed for the bus.

The following six mornings the kids got up before the roosters sounded off! They rose, had their quiet times, and ate their breakfasts more quickly each day. Their hearts beat with God's heart for Agua Viva, pulling them into heartfelt and Spirit-led service and ministry born of love and relationship.

Although it was back-breaking work, they persevered as crude cinder blocks shredded gloves and tore skin in suffocating 119° heat, day after day. Yet only one thought throbbed in their hearts—*finishing*.

Paul's words to Timothy kept coming to life all week: I've fought the good fight, I have finished the course, I've kept the faith" (2 Timothy 4:7). It was a verse these young people would claim as their own by day seven.

Cement was slapped on the last block, and we all headed to the chapel. Several men picked up guitars and, with Raul, they knelt next to a roughly hewn podium. The rest of us reverently filed in and knelt, too. Exhausted and dirty and thrilled with the feeling that costly service gives, we filled the floor space, shoulder to shoulder, in humble adoration. One by one, fervent silent prayers found voice, and praise and thanksgiving filled the small structure. As the Spirit led, one guitar then another picked up a tune, and we worshiped, tears making muddy tracks down grimy faces—hearts forever melting together touching God's heart with honest, authentic worship.

I had often wondered how Moses felt when God told him, "Take off your shoes. You are standing on holy ground." That day. That worship. Those prayers with those men answered my question. We truly were kneeling on holy ground.

Prayers and praises finally subsided, and Raul gave a passionate message from Matthew 25 about feeding the hungry and visiting those in prison and giving water to the thirsty. He ended with a paraphrase of Jesus's powerful declaration, "To the extent that you've served and built rooms for these brothers of Mine, you've done it to Me." The men began to bless each of us by thanking us and pouring out their love for us in prayer.

Simply overwhelming. Tear tracks on every single face.

Mike took up a love offering for beds. "Just ask the Spirit what you're to give, and then give it. Let's ask Him now and listen." After about ten seconds, he passed his baseball cap through the chapel, and when it was all said and done, the men would soon have beds, too.

Saying good-bye was hard, and the kids struggled. God had certainly reshaped lives—again, and had totally changed priorities. The promised trip to the Mercado in downtown Juarez, once the greatest draw of this trip, was now rather ho-hum for the kids. But after quiet times and cereal, we boarded Pastor Gomez's well-used bus to give the kids a day at the giant market while he and his family cleaned our bus for our trip home.

The older kids paired up with younger ones, making sure all were accounted for and then dashed and scattered, bartering for treasures. We met for lunch, and they scattered for the last time, leaving various "treasures" in our charge. We grabbed a quick dinner at the Mercado and re-boarded the faithful little bus that has served Pastor Gomez for decades.

After heads were counted, we proceeded out of Juarez just as the sun slipped past the horizon, painting the sky in wild oranges and pinks. The bus buzzed with electricity as the team shared their bargains with each other and snacks were freely passed throughout the bus. This one big family now made the first-day fights a very dim memory.

Suddenly, the tired bus chugged and jerked and died. I shot up an urgent, silent prayer, *"Oh, Lord! We're in the worst part of Juarez at night. Please bring this little bus back to life."* Mike headed out to raise the hood, and I engaged the kids, "Let's take some time to pray." They immediately grabbed hands and began asking God for favor.

Another breakdown. What on earth will God do this time? I wondered silently.

Thirty minutes later, Mike shook his head and told us we had two choices. We could walk to the nearest church or stay on the bus and hope for help. Once again, I addressed the kids, "Let's ask the Lord about these two options."

I waited a minute or two and prayed with them for God's plan.

"Okay, how many think the Lord said to stay on the bus?" Several hands were raised. "And those for walking? Okay, we're going to stay on the bus." Just like that, all the older kids took the seats by the windows, moving their younger teammates to the inside seats where they would be safer.

Brad, one of the leaders, started strumming a song in the back of the bus, and I followed him on my guitar in the front of the bus. "He is holy. He is mighty. He is awesome in His power. He has risen. He has conquered. He has beaten the power of death. Alleluia, we will rejoice. Alleluia, we will rejoice."

Next time, louder.

Next time, louder and stronger.

Next time, way beyond just words.

It was a declaration of God's character. "*You* are holy. *You* are mighty. *You* are awesome in *Your* power. *YOU* have risen. *You* have conquered. *You* have beaten the power of death." It was a personal proclamation of faith, not sung *about* Him but sung *to* Him, as if face-to-face. Again and again the team reached the heavens with worship, and once again God responded.

The little bus jumped to life! The "Alleluia, we will rejoice" was raucous now and would propel this tired bus home. We finally pulled up in front of Pastor Gomez's church, and the faithful little bus died, never to come alive again. God proved Himself to this wonderful team, responding to their faith. Oh, what a ride home—maybe on the wings of eagles, as it says in Exodus 19.

One group left Louisville. Another returned, forever changed.

"BEYOND WORDS" – FOR DEEPER THOUGHT . . .

1. When have you been in a place of great need where circumstances stretched you? What did you gain from the experience?

2. Luke 10:1 recounts how Jesus sent His followers out two by two into the cities and places He would soon be. How could you make yourself available to be sent out by the Lord?

3. In Isaiah 6, Isaiah talks about seeing the Lord high and lifted up, sitting on a throne. The angels around the throne are saying, "Holy, Holy, Holy, is the Lord of hosts, the whole earth is full of His glory." Isaiah is overwhelmed and says, "Woe is me . . . I'm a man of unclean lips." An angel touches his lips with a coal from the altar and tells him, "your iniquity is taken away and your sin is forgiven." Immediately, Isaiah hears the Lord say, "Whom shall I send, and who will go for us?" Isaiah responds, "Here am I. Send me!" Record your thoughts on this amazing passage.

4. What door might the Lord open for you if you were to say, "Here am I. Send me!"? There is great need all around us. How might the Lord use you to make a difference? Whom could you serve, making their lives better and forever changing yours?

5. When has your worship been so sweet that you felt you were standing on holy ground? How did you respond?

6. If you've never experienced that kind of worship, what could you do to make it possible?

Beyond Words

To be crucified with Christ, I come to my cross.
It's a fiery struggle, and it's very long. Oh, my
Lord, come and strengthen me.
It's the crucified life. To be crucified with Christ.
Come and die and you will live.
(Galatians 2:20; Mark 8:34–35)

I'll Call You Grace

I was born and raised in Denver, and I had *never* been "down there." No one wanted to go "down there." But that is where we had been invited by the pastor of an inner city church and, for some reason that totally eluded me at the moment, I had said, "Yes, we'd love to come." Sure, I'd been to Czechoslovakia as a missionary six months after Communism's iron grip had been broken, but that was several years ago. And yes, I'd taken scores of kids to Juarez, Mexico, but we worked in a safe little Colonia outside the city. *This is definitely not the same. This is inner city Denver.*

I paced as I waited for everyone to arrive at our last missions meeting in preparation for our week down there. I had gathered a bunch of kids—most were students of mine, but some were sons and daughters of friends from church. I loved each one . . . and now wondered what I had been thinking because worry about the safety of these kids had been gnawing at me lately. I had even asked the Lord to keep them home if they were not to do this. Then, slowly, deliberately, I brought each one of them before the Lord and begged for their safety, for the Lord to surround each one as a shield.

Scuffling feet and wild chatter interrupted me as most of the youth group burst into the room, energized, expectant, and thrilled to be part of this mission team. I rose to greet them and Linda, my co-leader, and let a long slow sigh slip through pursed lips. Linda is a wonderful woman with a zest for life, for others, and for the Lord. We only caught snippets of time together as I taught Language Arts full-time, and she and her husband Ray were raising three boys and working full-time.

Hugs and hellos and more hugs. How I loved these kids— mostly seventh-graders, but some high schoolers, too—young adults really. I quickly counted heads, nodded at Linda, and we began the meeting. One by one, we covered our list of thirty-three items, mostly what *not* to bring, causing a chorus of groans and moans. We paused for questions and clarifications and then huddled together to pray.

"We leave tomorrow morning at 9:30," I reminded them. "You *all* need to be here at 9:00. Okay?" Everyone nodded except Lisa, her brow wrinkled into a tight frown. "Lisa, what's up?"

"Well, I'm just wondering . . . I mean, I guess . . . well, I dunno . . ."

I could sense deep concern but couldn't help her find the words to express it.

"Lisa?"

"Well, Ms. L., what exactly are we going to do *down there*? Like, will we do different things each day or what?"

Bull's-eye! Lisa's "down there" hit the place where my own reservations rumbled. *Down there.* Anxiety twisted my stomach into a tight knot. I hadn't collected the words to explain the tumultuous rumblings within me. Was it fear, and I simply needed to have faith? Was it the Lord telling us not to go? Telling *me* not to go? Should someone else help lead this trip? *It's not too late to make some changes. But should I?*

But I did nothing . . . and . . . well, sure enough, all thirteen of them showed up on time the next morning. We piled into two vans and headed "down there," my anxiety still sharp.

Bubbling with excitement, Pastor Rob met us and showed us our two rooms in the back of his little church building. Rooms full of bunk beds with skinny aisles and barely enough space for our basic bags. The kids now saw the wisdom in the "do-not-bring" list. We wolfed down a small lunch and waited for Rob to take over. With infectious enthusiasm, he gave us a general outline of what the week would hold and then led us on a tour of the neighborhood. It was full of sights that hurt the soul: squalor, winos in gutters, children in rags, empty eyes—too much for the senses. I watched the kids and prayed for them and for those we saw.

Sobered and silent, we headed back to the church, where Rob cared for us. He let us share our shock, cry our tears, and ask our questions. Then he shared his heart for the neighborhood, and God's heart for the people. He led us in worship and in prayer. The kids poured out their hearts, asking the Lord to use them and spend them and give them divine appointments. They prayed that they would make a difference *down here.*

My concerns diminished, at least for a time. God was already at work, and I just knew that He had great things in store for us. We ate a small meal together, and no one needed a push to head to bed, get rest, and be ready for God to use them the next morning.

Rob packed our first four days full. We fed hundreds of homeless people, sitting with them, visiting, laughing, and loving them. The kids asked them for their stories and told them about Jesus. We listened. We cared. We worked at an orphanage cleaning, painting, and playing; the team told Bible stories to anyone who gave them an ear. We scoured the neighborhood, knocking on doors, asking if there was a need we could meet, giving Bibles to all who showed an interest.

The highlight for us was the debriefing time each evening after our meal. No wonder God brought these youngsters *down here*. He was growing them up in Him. Changing them. Filling them with His heart for the inner city world so vastly different than their own.

Much bolder with each new day, we listened as Rob explained our next mission: Go two-by-two *down there*—East Colfax—and expect a divine appointment. My breath caught in my throat. Linda shot me a glance that said she agreed. Not into the neighborhood today, but down to East Colfax. Not the place to take kids. I mean, *I* didn't even want to go. Anyone who lived in Denver avoided East Colfax.

I hit a crossroad. Walk in faith or walk in common sense? For me, common sense was screaming a lot louder than the whisper of faith.

Rob dismissed the kids into their quiet time spots, something we did for an hour each morning after breakfast to seek God's will for the day, then he immediately met with Linda and me.

"Rob, I don't feel good about this," I said. He nodded but didn't speak. We both looked at Linda. Her youngest son was with us, so her opinion really counted.

"Well, I'm uneasy too. However, we've prayed for safety and for God's Kingdom to come in these kids and in those we meet down here."

Rob nodded but still didn't speak. We bowed our heads. All I could get out was, "Lord, have Your way."

Just then, Jon, one of my seventh-graders, slipped into our circle. "Amen, Ms. L. Amen. We didn't do quiet time. We prayed as a team. We're supposed to do this."

So we would go out two-by-two, up and down East Colfax, trusting the Lord to give us divine appointments. Each pair had money to buy three lunches. At least one lunch had to be for someone on the street. We were to meet at 2:00 p.m. back at the church. Holding hands, we prayed just one prayer. "Lord, have *Your* way."

Linda and I returned from the streets before the rest of the team, filled with awe at how God matched us with sheep that so needed the Shepherd. Bristling with anticipation to hear the kids' stories, we turned our attention to praying them in. We counted each head with increasing sighs of relief.

It was almost 2:30, and we were still missing Jon and Eric. The jitters hit. On our knees, we all lifted Jon and Eric to the Lord, resolutely refusing to give fear a toehold. Oh, the intercession of the kids! Passionate. Authentic. A sweet aroma around the throne of God. The tardy duo finally burst through the door around 3:00, apologizing but gushing with a wild story of God's grace for three men they had found in an alley.

An alley! Yikes! Oh My Lord! My heart pounded with every detail. It was a divine appointment none of us would ever forget.

Just as passionately, each pair shared their amazing stories of God's great work. These youngsters were forever changed, and what a total rush for me! Sure, I loved having them in my Language Arts class, and my heart beat like a proud parent when they excelled. But doing faith with them, living with them while touching lost souls on East Colfax? No words for *that*!

Our worship time that evening touched heaven. We lingered long. As the clock inched toward midnight, Rob stood up and soberly gathered our attention. Something was up. I could see it in his eyes.

"We watched God work today in amazing ways. We found His heart and did His will today. However, the night down here needs more light than the day. I believe we are to go into the streets tomorrow night and follow His lead the same way we did today."

The night "down here." The words stung me. These kids on East Colfax at night!

Silence. Still basking in the warmth of worship and our successful day, Rob was asking more of us. I thought of the young man in Mark 10. He told Jesus he'd kept the commandments from his youth, and he seemed to feel pretty good about that. Then Jesus asked him for more. "Go sell all you have and give it to the poor and come follow Me." The young man went away grieving because he owned much, and Jesus did not go after him.

Heading out today two-by-two to buy someone a lunch had forced all of us well beyond our comfort levels. Now we'd been challenged to more, just like that young man. But these were kids. Kids I loved with parents whom I loved. *Oh, Lord, really? Is this Your heart and call to go further? Onto East Colfax? At night?!*

Silence.

"Let's ask the Lord," Linda said. "Right now, let's each ask Him if this is His call for us."

After some time, we went around the room, getting feedback from each team member. Not one dissenter.

"Ms. L?" Lisa timidly broke in. "I think we should, like, fast tomorrow to, like, prepare our hearts for the night's mission. Like, at least anyone who wants to, and we should, like, be quiet during the day too."

Out of the mouth of babes . . .

Heads nodded, and so it was. The next morning, Rob set out cereal for the team, then cheese and crackers for lunch. The gentle hum of a group of young people seeking the Lord filled the day. Quiet conversations. Singing. Small groups praying. A guitar here and there. Bible study. A small group of young believers caught up in Jesus's call for more.

Available and willing. Amazing.

We shared a very small meal that evening, and then Rob got his guitar and gathered us together to worship. We also served each other communion and asked the Lord to use us.

"Amen," Rob closed, and we headed down to East Colfax at midnight.

Packed bars. Wild music. Blaring sirens. Flashing lights here and there. Young people being thrown out of a raging concert, high on something. Police struggling with them, cuffing them. Drunks being thrown out of various establishments. Prostitutes soliciting.

It was sensory overload!

We moved in a tight group, Rob in front, Linda in the middle, and I closing them in from behind. *Oh, how I wished the three of us were six or nine or more.* I was totally overwhelmed, worried about what these kids were hearing and seeing and about to see, asking God if we'd made a huge mistake, fighting fear, and begging for faith. For protection. For God's will and divine appointments.

Rob held up his hand and stopped us. Police cars screamed to a gay bar about 50 feet from us. A mob had formed to watch a filthy fight amongst a group that was thrown out of the bar. We huddled at the mouth of an alley to pray. Rob and Linda and I linked hands, enclosing our kids. Rob prayed aloud for this neighborhood. The kids prayed aloud for all kinds of things. I prayed for the kids—silently—for their hearts and senses that were being assaulted by the darkness surrounding us.

That's when it happened. That's when the Lord's divine appointment tapped me on the shoulder. I swung around, all the kids swinging around behind me, their frightened breathing on my neck and shoulders.

"What the ____ are you doin' here?" she shouted, standing nose to nose with me. Her burning joint sent fumes into the group. Her "clothes" covered maybe three percent of her body. Her painted eyes were glaring and hateful.

"We're praying, ma'am. We're Christians."

"Ma'am? Idiot. Do I look like a ma'am to you? I'm an East Colfax whore!"

I put my hand out. "I'm Kathy. What's your name?"

She spit on me and slapped my hand away.

"Like I'd give you my name. Whore's don't use names."

"Well, I'll call you Grace, then."

"_____! There's no grace here! Look around, stupid. And Praying? ____!" she swore.

The joint was just a nub beginning to burn into her fingers. I tried to touch her, telling her it was going to burn her, and she freaked. Swearing. Cursing. Slapping my hand. "Whores burn every night! Every night! We deserve to burn!"

"Grace, no! God loves you."

"What? Are you _____ deaf? I am an East Colfax whore! God hates whores!"

"Grace, if God can love me, He can love you."

"Yeah, right! What the _____ would you know about that? Are you a whore?"

There it was. Did I come clean or save face with my students? I was their teacher, their mission's leader, their model of

Christianity. But this desperate woman, Grace, stood before me by God's appointment.

"Well, Grace, I've lived a sinful life, too, and I know God loves me."

"You've been a whore? A whore! Don't you get it? There's nothing lower," she spat.

"Well, no, I've not been a whore, but . . ."

"But nothin,' you_____ Christian!" Hate for her lifestyle and herself oozed from her like venom.

"Grace," I insisted, offering her my hand again, "I've lived in gay bars as a lesbian. I've lived in sexual sin. I've tried to kill myself. I hated my lifestyle and myself. I know shame. I know pain. I thought I couldn't get free, so I decided to take my life."

She said nothing, but she slowly, cautiously took my hand, her defenses weakening.

"Grace," I repeated, "God stopped my suicide attempt and gave me His forgiving grace. His death on the cross paid for all my sin. It pays for yours, too. Turn to Him, ask Him, and He'll give you grace. He'll forgive you too."

Fighting tears, still trying desperately to be tough, she responded. "I have a son I have to support. This is all I know. There's no way out."

"Just tell Him that. He will give you a way out. He loves you, Grace." I inched toward her to hug her. For an instant I thought she might let herself be loved—the right way—but she stiffened.

"Get out! Get out, you _____ Christians!" she screamed as she bolted into the blackness of the alley.

"God loves you, Grace!" I yelled as I watched her run away.

"God loves you, Grace," the team echoed, staring after her.

We spent another hour on the streets, huddling to pray here and there. One by one, each of the kids found his or her way to me, hugging me, thanking me for bringing them on this trip.

God had His way on East Colfax that week. He asked us for more, and He gave us more. He gave us Grace.

"I'LL CALL YOU GRACE" – ## FOR DEEPER THOUGHT . . .

1. How often do you get out of your comfort zone to stretch yourself or to reach out? What could you do to stretch yourself?

2. Have you ever asked the Lord to give you a divine appointment? What would need to change within you to venture out in this way so that He could use you?

3. How important is your reputation to you? How honest and authentic are you able to be about your weaknesses? How might God use your honesty and authenticity to encourage someone else?

4. In John 8, when Jesus met the woman who had been caught in adultery, her sin totally exposed, He said, "I do not condemn you. Go. From now on sin no more." How does this encourage you? What sin in your life might you need to expose to Jesus so He can forgive you?

5. Romans 8:1 states, "Therefore there is now no condemnation for those who are in Christ Jesus." What thoughts go through your mind as you read this verse? What does it mean to be "in Christ Jesus?"

6. Is there anything in your life that perhaps once shamed you but can now be used to encourage someone else because it's been confessed and forgiven? How could you encourage someone because of what you've gone through?

7. Have you ever felt as if you don't deserve God's grace? What has caused you to feel that way? Jeremiah 32:17–18 says, "Ah Lord GOD! Behold, You have made the heavens and the earth by Your great power and by Your outstretched arm! Nothing is too difficult for You, who shows lovingkindndess to thousands . . ." How does this encourage you to tell the Lord your need and receive His grace?

8. Matthew 25 records Jesus teaching His disciples. He says when He was hungry, they fed Him; when thirsty, they gave Him a drink; when He was a stranger, they invited Him in; when in prison, they visited Him. The disciples didn't understand because none of these things actually happened. Then Jesus gave them the punch line. "Truly I say to you, to the extent that you did it to one of these brothers of Mine, even the least of them, you did it to Me." How does this encourage you to reach out to others and meet their need? Where could you begin to take action?

I'll Call You Grace

The Almighty saving the lost.
The Almighty hanging on the cross.
The Almighty coming to earth.
The Almighty giving us worth.
We are but dust made in Your image.
We have hearts of stone. You are perfect love.
(John 3:16; Ezekiel 11:19)

Cradled

The warm summer weather is just beginning to slide into fall at the cabin in the Colorado Mountains. This changing of the seasons invites all the regulars and some I've never even seen before to come out and show themselves. Each day is a kaleidoscope of life—theatrical entertainment of the simplest, purest kind.

The opening act takes place each morning at the birdbath. The first full-breasted robin to step into the water exhibits a modicum of decency as it gracefully and gradually begins dipping its wings into the cool liquid. When time comes to wash the tail feathers, however, all discretion is abandoned.

Water shoots up and out and over in all directions. What was once clearly a robin now looks like a mass of frenzied feathers caught in a wild, wet whirlwind. And how could it possibly be better?

Add more robins! Two. Three. Sometimes even four. They are like toddlers in a kiddie pool smacking tiny palms on still water, squealing with delight, sending water in every direction. The spectacle always triggers hearty laughter. And they are not alone. Throughout the day, scores of birds of all shapes, sizes, and colors bathe and drink, filling my heart with a quiet awe of the Creator and His creation, softening the struggles of my yesterdays and the weight of my tomorrows as Mom and Dad's full-time caregiver.

Rivaling "water world" or the "extreme sports" enthusiasts—two small squirrels, their tummies dazzling white against their deep-gray bodies, their BB-black eyes encircled in a thin white band like glistening mascara perfectly applied—scamper out of and over and around the boulders behind the cabin. They then jet up the closest tree and fling themselves from tree to tree like tiny Tarzans. As the branches bend, I half expect them to snap back and whip the little rascals through space. But they tenaciously cling to each branch, then race out to the very tip, snatch a small green pinecone, and then reverse the process as if completing time trials at Daytona. Nest building? Food storage? One can only guess.

Sometimes, however, the little handmade feedbox hanging from one limb changes their course, and the little scamps become picky, yet uniquely polite, diners. With their bushy tails tucked up and over their rounded backs, they reach into the box, grab a sunflower seed, and then turn back toward the opening. With two or three precise bites, they swallow the seed, letting the shells float to the ground, keeping the "kitchen" nice and tidy.

These little creatures are doing what needs done for the coming winter with urgency and a focus that affect admiration and a quiet contentment that things are as they should be.

Not to be outdone, the ground creatures also pulsate with activity. Baby chipmunks, dozens of them, play tag. There are streaks of stripes. Hiding. Seeking. Chasing. Darting up and down and back and forth. They tumble over each other, creating miniature whirling dervishes in the dirt. Stopping only momentarily as if to squeak a warning, *"Ready or not, here I come"* or *"You're it."*

The second the squirrels vacate the feedbox, the bigger chipmunks hit it, packing their pouches like overstuffed luggage for a long winter. During "tag" time-outs, the little ones snatch whatever food falls out of the box and resume their play.

The blue jays strut to and fro, regally cloaked in their iridescent blue robes, their feathered top notches wiggling around like loose wigs, making it clear that they are next.

Smaller birds don't make their approach if the blue jays are holding court, and watching the little ones come and go is like watching fireworks—spots of colors splashing the air. Exploding bursts of brilliant white tail feathers flash here, patches of sunshine-yellow necks there, and occasionally glimpses of blood red. Endlessly unique. Fully wonderful.

Eventually, dusk descends and fiery oranges, pinks, and reds dance through heaven's blues and whites. Then, that unique mountain silence quietly announces the finale.

Elegant white-tailed deer begin tiptoeing down the rock path as if in a stately parade. They are powerful yet gentle creatures, alert ears cocking this way and that, sensitive to every noise no matter how slight, horns clad in velvet, coats thick for the coming snows. Their eyes reflect placid pools of deep brown, quietly surveying the scene. Unabashed, they feed on my plants and flowers and then mosey into the darkening woods.

I sit and watch an endless variety of God's creation taking care of business and bringing me into their simplicity and serenity. And tomorrow will bring a similar performance outside my picture window.

Then suddenly a "pop" on the window startles me. I have heard it before. I bolt for the nearest door and jerk to a stop beside a huge pot of petunias sitting on the deck just below the picture window of our mountain cabin, dreading what I might find, remembering the last time—the little grave I made under the protective arms of a ponderosa pine and how I watered the freshly dug earth with my tears.

I kneel before the pot of petunias, parting them gently, searching for the bird that had hit the window and fallen, hopefully into a pillow of flowers.

My shaking hands find him. He is a tad bigger than a sparrow wing tips laced with radiant white and a body blanketed in three tones of blended browns with threads of black running over his head and into his wings. Beautiful. Helpless. Hurt.

I feel not a single movement as I scoop him up and cradle him in my hands. One eye is closed. One is open but is blinking in odd rhythms. My tears sprinkle the petunias as I stroke his tiny head and whisper to him, urging him to be okay, begging God to heal the little guy.

Suddenly, his entire little body trembles, and he falls over onto his side. "No. No, God. Please. No." I pace and plead with him and God. "Come on, little one. Come on. You can do it. Oh, Lord, please help this little guy."

Still stroking his tiny head, I stumble toward the ponderosa pine to make another grave. On the way, however, the Lord's voice breaks through my sorrow, arresting my full attention.

"My eye is on the sparrow."

"Yeah," I sighed. "I've heard that song. That wonderful old hymn, which is seldom sung in our new age of 'modern' music," I replied sadly.

"No . . . No . . . My eye is on the sparrow," more insistent this time.

There is a rending inside as my spirit and soul collide.

"Listen, My child. This is how I cradle you. This is how I wrap My hands around you and weep and whisper and hurt when you hurt, when you hit an obstacle and fall. This is how I long for your healing. This is how I coax you to new life—different life, abundant life! My eye is on the sparrow, on you, just like your eye is on this helpless one."

In an instant, the simple words, *My eye is on the sparrow,* are turned into *rhema,* into *revealed* truth, as I glimpse God's heart. My desperate ache for this small bird is His desperate love for me! My tears are His tears!

I fall to my knees but not to make a grave. I fall to listen, to be still as the eternal touches the temporal, as the infinite teaches the finite.

A deep pause in the pulse of life.

Barely aware of my feathery friend in my hands, I am startled beyond words when his entire body quivers, and he gets back on his feet. I open my hands a bit, and two beady, black eyes stare back, blinking in perfect unison. Overwhelmed, I scurry to find a place to un-cradle him, a place where his tiny feet can find safe, solid ground. I laugh out loud at his short hops and the precarious first fluttering of his wings, wondering how much I look just like that after I fall. I sense a chuckle from the heavens, too. Gathering courage, the little guy springs forward.

We have liftoff! *Oh, Lord, we do have liftoff.*

"CRADLED" – FOR DEEPER THOUGHT . . .

1. King David wrote this in Psalm 139:4–5, 13 (NIV): "Before a word is on my tongue you know it completely. You hem me in behind and before, and you lay your hand upon me. . . . For you created my inmost being; you knit me together in my mother's womb." How does it encourage you to hear how intimately the Lord knows and loves you? How will these truths change the way you go about your day-to-day life?

2. In Matthew 10:30–31 Jesus says, "But the very hairs of your head are all numbered. So do not fear; you are more valuable than many sparrows." What does this tell you about how intimately God knows you?

3. In Matthew 6:8 Jesus says, ". . . your Father knows what you need before you ask Him." Think about all your needs. Then think about the marvelous truth of this verse. Your Father knows each one of your needs before you even mention them to Him. How does this change the way you perceive your needs?

4. In Luke 12:24 Jesus says, "Consider the ravens, for they neither sow nor reap; they have no storeroom nor barn, and yet God feeds them; how much more valuable you are than the birds!" Think about this declaration from Jesus. How does that comfort you? How does it strengthen you?

5. In light of the verses above that declare you are "cradled" in His care and love and attention, what changes are you moved to make in your day-to-day life?

Cradled

Quiet the thoughts that bind you.
Quiet your fearful mind.
Quiet the storms inside you and know
that you are mine.
I see the tears you're cryin'. I see
you on your knees.
I hear your cry come to Me. My child,
I am pleased.
(Psalm 46:10, 56:8)

Give Me Ten More

Bam! In an instant, Mom's frail frame spasms—again. Her left arm tenses at odd angles, causing her arthritic fingers to stiffen and tighten and curl like small knobby twigs. Her left leg jerks out straight, stiff, off to the side, toes pointing like thin arrows. Her lips droop. Her chin sags. Tired brown eyes shoot out darts of terror as her brain struggles to form a simple syllable, any syllable, but is silenced by internal explosions.

I crash to my knees next to the couch and gather Mom into my arms. I search her eyes but can't find her. I can't reach beyond the eruptions in her brain.

"It's all right," I whisper, over and over and over. Desperate to believe it. Desperate to stop the attack. My heart bursting. Bursting for Mom. For Dad. For me. Just bursting!

Dad kneels too, and gently pats Mom's head, spilling tears but hushing fears too big to voice. Sixty-plus years of marriage.

What would he do without her? He looks at me and waits for wisdom, for answers, for direction. What would our Hospice nurse say? I have no answers.

"Shhhhh. It's all right," I repeat, patting the wrinkled skin of Mom's sagging cheek, her eyes darting here and there, searching for something familiar. "It's okay. I think you're having a stroke. It's all right. We're right here." All the while I am the while silently screaming, *No! It's not okay! I'm here, but I'm helpless. Totally helpless. I can't do this, Mom. This is not okay!*

The terror in her eyes pleads with me, but I don't have what she needs. I'm searching my depths, but it's not there. All I find is a frantic battle. I'm straddling a chasm that is sucking me into its blackness. On one side, reason says, *"This could be the one that takes her. That would be a blessing. Let her go."* On the other side, insane emotions scream, *"Let her go? How? What will I do without her?"* The terror in her eyes shredding my heart, paralyzing me, crushing me like an angry vice.

Eventually, I sense a slight release of her muscles and wonder if it's real or imagined.

"Mom? Mom? Are you there?" Almost imperceptibly, a hint of recognition registers and slowly replaces the wild fear in her eyes. I see "Mom" again. She is back—her spirit reflected in the soft brown of her tired eyes.

"Wh – wh – a – a – t ha – pp – en – ed?" she stutters in squeaky, weak spurts.

Stroke number seven. Life redefined. Again.

"I think you had another stroke. It's okay. I think it's over."

Her left leg and arm are still stiff and heavy. Her fingers still bent in all kinds of odd angles. No! It's not okay!

I want the love in my eyes to strengthen and encourage her while my mind and heart are reeling. Hating what these strokes are doing to Mom; hating my inability to handle them more sensibly; hating the agony of the human condition as the body decays and rebels and inches towards death . . . slow death . . . death by degrees. Never knowing how many more will come. Never knowing when the next one will hit. Never prepared. Never ready. Never able.

"Wh – what hap – pened? I cou – couldn't ma – ake a word."

"I think it was a stroke, Mom. It's okay. We're here, and it'll be okay." It was a lie, but I couldn't think of anything else to say.

We stayed on our knees a long time, trying to find our way, groping for wisdom, for elusive stability, waiting for Mom to fully find herself, to find us, wondering what damage would remain, searching each other's eyes for hope and courage. Fighting to figure out what to do next.

No words. Just closeness. Intertwined. Thin threads, tightly knit together by desperation and heartache.

"I – I can m-make s-s-som-e word-s now I thin-k, bu-u-t-t my le-g won't wor-k."

"I know. It's okay, Mom. We'll figure it out," I say, cupping her thin face in my hands, urgently pouring love into her, fighting hot tears.

Her frightened eyes holding mine, searching for strength and reassurance.

"Ooo o-k-k-kay," she whispers, her "good" hand taking mine, squashing my fingers, her bony and bulging arthritic knuckles turning white with pressure. Tiny red-and-blue veins, like delicate lace, crisscross the back of her hand, almost shining through her translucent skin. Her seventy-four-pound body fights for life but fails . . . fails little by little, day by day . . . every day. I press her thin hand to my lips, desperate to help.

"Mom, I got-ta go, go make some . . . uh . . . phone calls," I stammer and hurry out of the room, trembling from head to toe, emotions tumbling like bingo balls in the hopper, dammed tears crashing through.

Clinging by a thread, I know I must keep my head, but I'm bursting, flying apart in shattered fragments—fighting to keep it together. *I don't know how to do this. Mom! I don't know how to watch you disintegrate like this.* My own terror keeps rising, stealing my breath.

"Just pick up the phone. We need a wheelchair," I blurt—to no one.

Somehow, that breaks my panic and buys me a few seconds of sanity. I force myself into long, deep breaths, praying that my head clears, begging the Lord for wisdom and the courage that Mom believes I have.

Phone calls made; a wheelchair arrives. Primary Care Provider. Hospice. Senior care coordinator. Physical therapy. Occupational therapy. A bedside commode.

Next.

We move Mom into the bedroom, closer to the bathroom. Dad and I scramble, figuring it out second by second. "Okay, Mom, use your good leg to push—I'll lift your left leg. Dad, you lift her from the waist, and we'll lower her onto my computer chair with rollers. Dad, you push and hold her steady. I'll carry the left leg. Okay, I'll brake the front wheels and carry the leg. You brake the back wheels while you help her onto the bed."

"Okay, I'll . . . and you can . . . and Mom . . . then I . . ." on and on it went until she was snug in her cuddly duds, as she calls them, and safely tucked in bed.

My mind raced and worked and planned and wondered all night long. The minutes of the next two days crawled by as we persistently fought to figure out how to handle the physical demands of the simplest tasks . . . simple that is, until this stroke. None of us were prepared for the emotional upheaval we faced. While Mom's left arm and hand slowly recovered, her left leg remained totally paralyzed, and we all three bounced between faith and fear, tears, and silence—all intertwining in wild, senseless patterns.

Then, on the third day, our lives were forever changed, again.

Conchetta arrived. Actually, she had four names when she introduced herself, all of them *very* Italian. But all I could remember was Conchetta. An imposing figure, she was five foot two, maybe, but thick and strong, with a presence that made us want to salute when she spoke.

Within seconds, we were all gathered around Mom's bed, and Conchetta began the physical therapy assessment. A sudden wave of relief swept over me, and my own taut muscles loosened a bit. Conchetta was in control now. I was "off duty"— almost like a plug had been pulled and the piled-up tension began melting and draining. Things really hadn't changed, but reinforcements had come. Conchetta's strength somehow flowed toward and into me as she worked with Mom's arms and legs.

I forced my breaking heart into momentary submission and grabbed paper and pencil to take notes. I knew my scrambled brain would remember nothing, so I riveted my eyes on Conchetta's every movement and scribbled down every action so that we could repeat the PT in the days and months, maybe years, to come.

"Marty, lift your knees," Conchetta ordered. "Lift your knees."

Yikes! She's sure not very nice, I thought.

"Lift your knees. Now! Now, Marty!"

"Hey!" I blurted.

Conchetta thrust her open palm toward me like an iron stop sign and shot me a look that silenced me.

Mom's right knee obeyed.

"Now, give me ten more. Lower it and lift it ten more times. Now, move the left leg." Mom strained and worked. Nothing happened.

"Marty, try harder!" Conchetta demanded.

Mom grimaced, fighting to flex unresponsive muscles.

"Marty, move that leg!"

The tiniest waver went through the muscles of the limp leg.

"Give me ten more. Now."

What the . . .! This woman is heartless!

Dad's body tensed. Breathing fast. Anger rising.

Just in time, she changed gears.

"Let me help," Conchetta encouraged, as she lifted Mom's left knee and leaned in toward her just in time to stop its total outward flop.

"Push against my tummy, Marty. Push."

Nothing.

Placing her hand on the inside of Mom's knee, she commanded "Push, Marty! Harder! Push against my hand!"

Another slight tremor in Mom's muscles.

"Give me ten more, Marty. Ten more, Marty. Now!"

My emotions, twisting me like a pretzel, came to crisis point. I stood, intending to show Conchetta the door, when I heard the Lord's still, small voice say, *"Sit down and watch Me work."*

But, Lord, I countered silently, *she's mean! Mom's not done exercises for decades, and this woman's pushing her way too hard. And Mom's just had her seventh . . .*

"Watch Me work," I heard again.

Slowly, I surrendered, sat down, and fought to refocus.

After almost an hour of pushing Mom, which to me seemed more like punishing Mom, Conchetta asked if she could make it to the kitchen in her little transfer chair.

Mom whispered a weak, "I think so," and Conchetta helped her out of bed and into the chair. Not a wheelchair. Just a chair with four small wheels and two thin handles. Dad or I had been pushing Mom in it while one of us would lead, holding up her limp leg. We headed for the chair to help. Conchetta jumped in front of us, bumping us backward, blocking us.

"Marty, move yourself to the kitchen sink," she barked.

Anger and blood surged into Dad's face, and my mouth dropped open in total shock.

Mom glanced at us, pleading, begging for help, but Conchetta stood between us and Mom like a stone-cold wall. Why we didn't fight her, I don't know. It's like she immobilized us—like she incapacitated us somehow.

"Start, Marty! Get yourself to the kitchen sink!"

Mom pulled with one leg while thrusting her body weight forward, desperately inching her way across thick carpet. "Ten more! Just like that. Give me ten more!"

Eight minutes. Fifteen. Twenty minutes later, Mom had moved less than three feet and was gasping for air, tears trickling down her wrinkled cheeks.

My heart thumped violently. I tore my eyes from Mom as tears exploded and poured over my cheeks. *Lord!* I silently screamed. *Why are You allowing this? Why?*

Dad snapped! He pushed around Conchetta and grabbed a chair handle. Conchetta met his challenge, snatched his hand, and jerked it off the handle. She grabbed his other hand and locked them in hers. His eyes flashed with anger—and hurt. He hit her with hot words. "How dare you tell me what to do! Over sixty years of marriage. I *will* help her! This is way too hard for her and you know it!"

My breath caught in my throat. I prayed he wouldn't hurt Conchetta. Mom slumped forward and wept. I wept. Conchetta didn't budge. She steadily held Dad's fierce stare.

Just then, I heard the Lord again. *"She knows Marty can and must do this."*

I patted Dad's shoulder and pulled him toward me. "It's okay, Dad. Really."

Conchetta knelt next to Mom, one arm around her bony, rounded shoulders, her other hand gently wiping Mom's tears. "Marty, if you are ever going to regain use of your leg, you *must* exercise now. Okay? Sympathy will keep you crippled."

My thoughts raced, *Oh, Lord, that's true, huh? My sympathy would cripple Mom!*

Still comforting Mom, Conchetta turned to Dad. "Ralph, I understand you love Marty. The only way to help her is to put your hands in your pockets."

"Bu . . ."

"No buts. You want your wife to walk again. I do, too. You must trust me."

Mom squeaked out a tiny, "I think I can do this," and began inching her way to the sink. Conchetta rose and gently slipped Dad's hands into hers. They inched along just behind Mom, and Conchetta began quietly coaching Dad on what to do and what not to do once they got to the sink.

Thoroughly spent, I eased into a chair at the dining room table and let my head fall into my cupped hands. The rhythmic ticking clock soothed my soul. Jeremiah 12:5 slid into my consciousness. "If you have run with the footmen and they have tired you out, Then how can you compete with the horses?" I poured my thoughts out to the Lord in response to the Spirit's teaching.

Oh, my Lord. This is what You meant when You told me to watch You work. I am tired, and sympathy would cripple me too, wouldn't it? You know that. You know that I have to exercise my faith muscles now. That I must "give You more" and then more and then more. You know what's coming. You know the faith it will take to stand during the fierce shaking that's ahead. Just like Conchetta knows the battle we're facing with the paralysis of this stroke—and perhaps the next stroke and the next one. Conchetta's "give me ten more" is the only way for Mom to recover from the paralysis. Oh, Lord, my sympathy would cripple both of us. Your sympathy would cripple us. Lord, I do want to be able to run with the horses.

They finished at the sink, and Conchetta helped us help Mom back into bed. She then wrapped her thick arms around Mom and held her. Tears fell freely from all four of us. She hugged Dad hard. Then me. "Regular physical therapy will begin day after tomorrow," she explained and then left.

That night, sleep eluded me for a long time as I stared out my north window at the stars. Matthew 6 came to my mind, how each day has enough trouble of its own. What an understatement!

I closed my eyes and replayed our time with Conchetta. Miraculous. A living parable, illustrated by the Lord in our very own home. God had said, "Watch Me work," and did He ever! Through Conchetta, He taught us why we must exercise faith in tests and trials for it to be strong and responsive.

I wasn't sure I could yet run with the horses, but I heard Him whisper, "Kathy, exercise your faith, my child, give Me ten more. Ten more for a faith that won't fail."

"Yes, my Lord. Yes," I whispered back and quickly sank into a deep, peace-filled sleep.

"GIVE ME TEN MORE" –
FOR DEEPER THOUGHT . . .

1. What challenges lie before you right now?

2. How can sympathy hurt someone? When have you reacted in sympathy when it wasn't the best thing to do? What would have been a wiser reaction?

3. When you are stretched beyond what you think you can bear, what do you do? To whom do you turn?

4. What situation have you faced already that tested and stretched your faith? In hindsight, how did you grow? What changes did the situation bring about in you?

5. James 1:2–3 says, "Consider it all joy, my brethren, when you encounter various trials, knowing that the testing of your faith produces endurance. And let endurance have its perfect result, so that you may be perfect and complete, lacking in nothing." How does this encourage you to press on? What strength do you gather from these verses?

6. 1 Peter 5:10 declares, "After you have suffered for a little while, the God of all grace, who called you to His eternal glory in Christ, will Himself perfect, confirm, strengthen and establish you." Record your response to this Scripture.

7. In what specific situation or trial do you need to "give God ten more" right now so your faith will grow?

Give Me Ten More

My child, be anxious for nothing. Each day has
trouble of its own.
Oh, my child, your Father knows just what you
need.
He is faithful, He is kind, He is just,
And each new mornin' brings His love.
(Lamentations 3:22-25; Matthew 6:25-34)

Stiff-necked

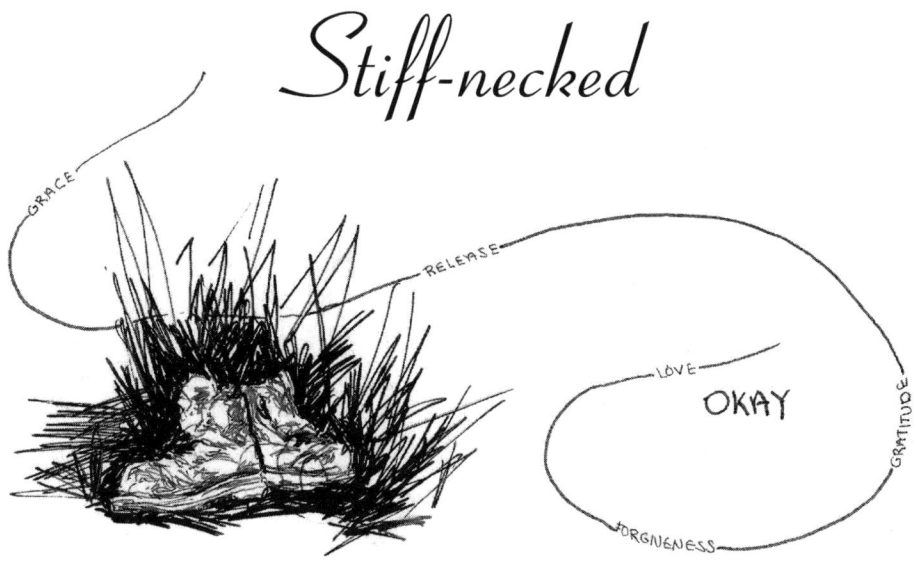

GRACE

RELEASE

LOVE

OKAY

GRATITUDE

FORGIVENESS

My tired, tight muscles had good reason to be angry. Mom was bravely battling severe health issues and needed a full-time caregiver, so I moved in with my folks after Mom's first stroke. She now weighed seventy-two pounds and was bedridden after suffering three surgeries, four lengthy hospital stays, eleven more strokes . . . and counting. I wondered how much more her frail body could endure.

At the same time, I was totally clueless that a deep desperation was choking me. It surfaced when Sue, our hospice social worker showed up and jolted my world. Under the guise of taking a tour of our gardens, when we stepped out the door, Sue turned, took my arm, and asked, "Kathy, what are you doing for *you*?"

A gush of tears answered. Torrents of anxiety, hurt, anger, weariness, and maybe a hundred other things surfaced. By degrees, great pressure was released with each sob. Sue wrapped her arms around me and gave silent permission to implode and, I guess, explode some, too.

Before she left, she ordered me to do something for myself, so I scheduled a massage and started counting down the days and hours before my appointment.

Massage day finally arrived, and the thirty-minute drive toward Blackhawk was therapeutic in itself as I stole glances at ranges of snowcapped mountains and meadows bursting with wildflowers. The Lord's great majesty was on display; His presence was palpable. My spirit and ears were on alert . . . listening. I smiled and thought about how we met, twenty-nine years earlier when He stopped my suicide attempt. I gave Him my life that night, and the next morning I opened the Bible for the first time. The words of the little boy Samuel, "Speak Lord, your servant is listening," changed my life. God spoke to Samuel that night, and I knew He would do no less for me, if I could learn to listen.

"Ahh, yes, Lord," I chuckled. "We've been talking with each other for many years now. Speak, Lord, I am still listening."

I pulled into Lena's driveway and exhaled slowly, fully embracing this break. I knocked on the door and instantly felt "off duty." This snippet of time held no responsibilities for me, just a life-giving break, like a soft shower on a dusty day.

I slipped under the sheet, closed my eyes, and disengaged. I was completely burden-free, if only for a short time. Quiet worship music began soaking through my exhaustion, lifting me, taking me beyond myself, beyond the pressures of life-and-death struggles and decisions.

Lena padded into the room and gently slipped her hands under my neck, cupping my head in her palms. I barely noticed that this wasn't her usual way of beginning a massage, but even that thought quickly drifted way.

In its place, a memory slowly unfolded. I saw myself in the kitchen where I grew up. A faint, fearful voice from within whispered, "Resist this," as if the kitchen held dark secrets. But I had no power to do so.

Ever so slowly, my head began moving toward my right shoulder, like some range-of-motion therapy. When it began the same movement toward the left, however, piercing pain stopped me as if a knife had been thrust between two vertebrae. A thought surfaced to ask Lena what she was doing, but it disappeared too quickly, and my head began the slow movement back to the right.

Time passed. Movement to the right was easy and free. Movement to the left jerked to sudden halts by sharp pain. *Just go with it,* I told myself. *Just go with it.*

My awareness heightened but without effort or struggle. No panic. No strain—as if I was watching a play unfold. I'm on the massage table but also in the kitchen with Mom, Dad, and Eddy, my older brother. Never in my fifty-some years had this memory come to mind.

So very odd.

Lord, have your way. Help me listen, I prayed silently.

My head drifted to the left, shooting pain through my neck.

His voice broke through with a clarity and urgency that startled me. *"Kathy, who is the pain in your neck?"*

"Dad!" I spat, as pain shot through my neck again.

"You need to forgive him."

Still aware of my head gently moving toward the right, aware of being supported by loving hands, I became conscious that the Lord was dealing with me—gently, but insistently.

"You need to forgive your dad," the Shepherd repeated.

"Do you see what he is doing?" I blurted out (or rather the "young Kathy" blurted it). I was about nine, Eddy eleven. "Don't you see?"

Then steel-toed boots came into focus. I heard sickening thuds. My breath came in asthmatic spurts as the memories clawed their way to the surface.

"Yes, I see," the Lord assured me.

Aware now of the peaceful movement of my head toward my right shoulder, I felt I was caught in two realities: one of peace and one of panic. My head drifted to the left, and the pain stabbed again.

"Then why don't you stop it? Why don't you *do* something?" I screamed. Suddenly, I knew it was Eddy being kicked. Sickening thuds! Over and over. I knew Dad wore those boots. I couldn't breathe. Gulping bits of air. Struggling to stay conscious.

"Stop," I gasped, turning from the terror.

"I did do something. I AM doing something."

My head moved freely to the right, and a gentle breeze caressed and filled me. I took long, deep breaths and let them ease out ever so slowly. The leftward movement began until that stabbing pain stopped it cold, again.

"Yeah! You *took* him! That drunk driver killed him! You took my big brother! My hero! You took my protector!" I ranted breathlessly, looking away in fiery anger, pain splitting the core of my being.

"I spared him from what was coming. He is safe now. He is with me."

Sweet glimpses of Eddy with Jesus cascaded into my mind like gurgling streams and tiny waterfalls all around me. Images I'd never seen before. Peace washed through me. I wanted to linger here, but the rhythmic movement began its leftward motion.

"But what about me? What about Dad? I *hate* him!" Guillotine pain now, as if the blade had severed my neck, shooting arrows of agony into every nerve, sucking the air out of my lungs, out of my life.

"I want you to forgive him, Kathy."

Before the Lord, I took a quick inventory. The memory of Dad's boots and Eddy and me in the kitchen was new, but it was just one of hundreds in which Dad had hurt all of us—in so many ways, in so many places. A multitude of memories flashed through my mind. Years upon years of abuse. There was no getting around it.

Yet, here was my Lord inviting me, urging me into forgiveness. After all, He had forgiven me. How could I do less?

Instantly, the Lord's tenderness covered me like one of Grandma's soft quilts.

How? I asked silently. *I can say the words, but how does that work? What does that look like in real life?*

Like a set change between acts of a play, I was lifted somewhere. Not to a place defined by things or location. Just a place. A place of keen awareness. A place of knowing, I guess. Knowing God had done something in my heart. As if huddling together with the Lord to tell Him a secret, I whispered, *"Dad, I forgive you."*

My head almost touched my right shoulder and easily moved to the left, almost touching that shoulder, too. Tears from a deep well flowed freely. *Thank You. Thank You. Thank You.* Over and over, I praised Him silently. *Thank you, Lord.* Gratitude coursed through me like living water through dead places.

I could never forgive Dad on my own, but by surrendering to Jesus, He could do it through me—changing my heart, giving me words, and helping me walk it out day by day.

I thought about God calling His people stiff-necked in the Old Testament. I thought about how often He pleaded with them to yield themselves to Him completely. I thought about the dire consequences they suffered in not surrendering.

Oh, Lord, surrender is always sweeter. Thank You. Thank You for speaking with me about this. I know, Lord, that if you bring me to it, You will bring me through it.

Distant rumbles of thunder outside gradually reached my ears, as well as the delightful tapping of gentle rain. Then came that smell. There's none like it. The smell of rain in the mountains invited me to fill my lungs again and again and again with the refreshing air. My lungs' capacity seemed to have greatly increased. I became aware of Lena's hands and opened my eyes.

"What just happened here?" I asked Lena.

"You'll have to tell me. All I know is that the Lord told me to support what He was going to do."

"You were turning my head, weren't you?" I asked, trying to piece things together.

"No. You were doing that. I was just supporting you and your head," she answered as she left the room.

Enveloped in a strange kind of wonderment and bewilderment, I dressed—puzzled, yet fully aware that a seismic shift had occurred. I met Lena in the kitchen, and over a cup of tea, I shared what the Lord had done. An odd urgency pressed me to be brief, however. There was a compulsion now that I didn't understand until we prayed. I *had* to get home and hug Dad. In fifty-eight years, I hadn't hugged him! And now there was an urgency to do so. I didn't understand that either, but I knew I *must* act on it immediately.

I thought of the ten lepers in Luke 17. Jesus told them to go and on their way they would be healed. So it would be with me.

I skipped out into the rain like a little lamb set free. God thundered His delight and threw darts of lightning here and there as if throwing a party. I imagined Eddy right beside him, tickled with my freedom, grinning from ear to ear. I turned up the song "Healing Rain" and sang and cried and laughed all the way home.

It was past eleven, and my folks were asleep, but as I opened the door from the porch into the cabin, a light flipped on in their bedroom. Dad shuffled out and stood by the bedroom door.

"Oh, Dad," I blurted, "I'm sorry I woke you."

"No, you didn't. I don't know what woke me," he mumbled, rubbing his sleepy eyes.

"Dad, I know *Who* woke you," I chuckled, tossing my jacket on the back of a chair. Nearly running to him, I wrapped my arms around him and held him. Poor man. I thought his pacemaker might explode.

"Dad," I declared, "do you know that I love you?" The strength in the affirmation surprised me. I can't imagine what it did to him.

He stood, arms at his sides, speechless, motionless. "Dad, I love you. You need to know that."

When I finally released him, without eye contact, he peeped, "Okay," and shuffled back to the bedroom. I smiled and wondered what he was thinking and feeling.

Nothing more was said about that evening, and we settled back into life, always wondering when the next stroke would hit Mom and if it would be the fatal one. Twelve times thus far, during each stroke, she had somehow managed to ask the same question, "Who will take care of Ralph?"

Automatically, and quite coldly, each time I had replied, "God will."

I had made it quite clear to my younger brother and sister that when Mom died, *they* would get Dad because I wanted nothing to do with him. After each hospital stay, I had firmly reminded them, "I cared for Mom. *You guys* get Dad."

But surrendering to the Lord and forgiving my dad had changed everything. Caring for him would be a foreign and steep path, but the *best* path because the Lord had put me on it.

I knew that Jesus, who reached me during that massage, would also teach me to walk in the miracle He had wrought in my heart that day. The miracle of forgiveness. The forgiveness Jesus won on the cross for us and sends through us to others— *if* we're willing.

Israel suffered dire consequences for being stiff-necked, and the Lord had saved me from the same fate. "Oh, Lord. Thank You for touching my stiff neck," I whispered to Him, moving freely and closer to Him and His heart of forgiveness.

"STIFF-NECKED" – FOR DEEPER THOUGHT . . .

1. In what areas of your life would you be described as being stiff-necked? For whom or what do you feel a stubborn, unrelenting hardness?

2. For whom do you carry resentment or anger? Whom do you need to forgive?

3. Jesus teaches His disciples how to pray in Matthew 6:5–12. Verse 12 says, "And forgive us our debts, as we also have forgiven our debtors." Jesus explains in verses 14 and 15, "For if you forgive others for their transgressions, your heavenly Father will also forgive you. But if you do not forgive others, then your Father will not forgive your transgressions." Record your thoughts about this teaching, including things for which you would like to be forgiven and how many times you think the Lord has already forgiven you.

4. It has been said that the one who harbors unforgiveness is a prisoner of his/her own making, and that unforgiveness is a slowly eroding cancer. What would change in you, in your soul, in your life?

5. Peter asks the Lord a question in Matthew 18:21. "Lord, how often shall my brother sin against me and I forgive him? Up to seven times?" Jesus answered, "I do not say to you, up to seven times, but up to seventy times seven" (Matthew 8:22). What do you think Jesus's point was in this answer? Do you think Jesus was actually setting a limit or was He inferring that we forgive "as many times as needed?

6. What business do you need to transact with the Lord? In what areas are you stiff-necked? 1 John 1:9 says, "If we confess our sins, He is faithful and righteous to forgive us our sins and cleanse us from all unrighteousness." Take some quiet time and tell the Lord about your sins, including the sin of unforgiveness. Ask Him to help you forgive anyone who has wronged you, so that you may be free. Record what happens as you do this now and in the weeks to come.

7. "Therefore humble yourselves under the mighty hand of God, that He may exalt you at the proper time, casting all your anxiety on Him, because He cares for you" (1 Peter 5:6–7). It is humbling to confess and forgive; but the cleansing and blessing that come from the Lord afterward are beautiful and wonderful. Write your thoughts about and reactions to this passage. Record the results that you experienced when you confessed and forgave.

Stiff-necked

I see the weight that you're carryin', and I see
you struggling; with the load.
I see the heartache in your soul, but I am at
work making you whole.
Come aside. Come aside. Come abide.
I am the Lord your God, and I have bought you
with a price.
And you are mine now, and I love you.
Come abide. Come aside. Come my Bride.
(John 15:4–7; 1 Corinthians 6:20)

It's About the Two-Year-Old

Weary from taking care of my Mom and Dad full-time, I seized the moment to escape the instant Lisa, our hospice CNA, hit the door. Not quite carpe diem, as I only had two hours, but I sure snatched them.

Mom always perked up when Lisa came to bathe her, but it was the bathing of the soul that mattered most. Bedridden from twelve strokes, bath day was life to Mom's broken body. She and Lisa would chat and laugh and cry and talk about all the things one can't share with family as one is dying.

For the longest time, only Lisa knew that the tissue up Mom's left sleeve was for her nose and the tissue up her right sleeve was for her tears. The lonely tears when no one was looking. The tears of slow death. Each stroke stealing from her . . . but not killing her.

All of us wanted Mom to be able to die at home, surrounded by love and faith and worship and the Word, but the pain and heartache in the dying process dammed up tears and fears in all three of us. How precious it was that Lisa's love and touch coaxed Mom's tears to spill while bathing her.

Lisa arrived one day, and we *all* perked up. Usually, Dad and I headed outside to do various projects, working off tension, talking about the great grief of watching Mom disappear by degrees.

But this day was different. I knew exactly how to use those two hours. My shoulders and neck screamed for attention, and my dear friend and chiropractor had an open spot.

So, when Lisa hit the door, I hit the road. It would be tight, time wise, but I looked forward to the forty-minute drive. I popped my favorite worship CD in and headed down the mountain, into the city. Losing myself in the music, I ached for the Lord's presence. For His comfort. My own tears dripped into my lap, while no one watched.

Maybe deep grief demands privacy.

Then *BAM!* A great pressure smashed my chest. I snapped my blinker on, hit the brakes, and jerked the wheel to the side of the highway. From sixty-five to zero in seconds. I slid the shifter into park and flipped the key to off. My head fell forward to the steering wheel.

Pain. Labored breathing. Pressure crushing my chest. Fear! Couldn't stop it.

"Lord!" I blurted with a tiny burst of breath. "Help me!"

Time passed. Cars passed. Thoughts of death came and went. Slowly, almost reluctantly it seemed, the pressure loosened its grip. My thinking inched its way toward sanity. I eased my seat back and slumped into its embrace, waiting for my heart rate to slow down.

"Lord, was that a heart attack?"

It's about the two-year-old, I heard in my spirit.

"Lord?"

Silence. Communion quiet. As if the Lord and I had left the highway and retreated into a place of Spirit, a place of revelation. I waited.

It's about the two-year-old.

"Lord, I thought we did that work," I countered, recalling the hideous spider dreams followed by a season of counseling. Then more dreams followed by more counseling. Each time, the Lord faithfully led me to godly men and women to walk me through the pain of my childhood. After twelve brutal yet wonderful years, I found myself at two years old, when the abuse began. The Good Shepherd leading, pouring out grace and healing. Holding me. Loving me.

"Lord, what do you mean?"

He answered in a series of thoughts that raced through my mind. Me. Two years old. Terrified when Mom left at night to go to work. Scared to be left alone with Dad. Desperate for Mom to stay.

"Oh, my Lord! We're not done yet, are we?" I cried, waiting for my chest to loosen.

"But, Lord, I don't understand. I thought I was past all of that when You helped me forgive Dad. What now? Please show me how to let go of Mom *and* my fear of being left with Dad. Please help me, Lord. The next stroke could rip her away any moment."

In that instant, the buzz of traffic resumed, as if God had pressed a heavenly pause/resume button. I glanced at my watch, startled that I still had time to cancel my appointment.

Slowly, I slid back onto the highway, took the next exit, and headed back up the mountain.

I had no clue what the Lord would do, but He *had* to do something to loosen my grip on Mom and the dread of being left alone with Dad. Terror still choked the two-year-old within.

Four days passed, rather uneventfully, yet as I laid on the bed next to Mom, reading aloud her favorite book, *Hinds' Feet on High Places*, God moved. We held hands and shared our favorite Scriptures. We talked about heaven and the rapture at meeting our Bridegroom, Jesus. We cried. We laughed. God held the fragile threads of our lives, weaving them into a priceless tapestry. Perhaps for the first time in our lives, we touched hearts. I mean, she had been a desperate young wife with three little kids, a full-time job, and a husband who drank. I was a terrified little girl in an abusive household where she couldn't protect me. We had simply "disconnected" decades back, each to our own despair—each to our own methods of coping.

A bond sprouted when Jesus rushed into my life, interrupting my suicide attempt on my twenty-seventh birthday. Just a few weeks later Mom gave her life to Christ as she watched God work miraculous changes in me. So, for thirty years we shared Christ—but never our hearts. I guess we just didn't know how. But here we were—many strokes later—loving each other in sweetness as best we could.

The next morning, however, agitation rocked her. She squeezed my hands, her arthritic knuckles whitening with the pressure, and she stared at me—peering, searching.

"Mom? What is it?" I whispered.

"What will Ralph do without me?" she stammered.

There it stood. Hospice had told us that Mom was hanging on for a reason. That, for her, something was left undone—a loose end that she needed tied up.

"Dad will be fine. God will take care of him," I answered, more coldly than I liked. I hadn't shared with her what the Lord had done on the massage table. In the past, I had not cared what happened to Dad, and while I had forgiven him, walking out that forgiveness was still in process. I was not at all sure that I would stay and care for him until he passed.

She lay motionless, still looking into my soul. Tiny tears began trickling over her wrinkled cheeks.

My throat tightened, and I fought my own tears. The old memories flooded me again. I never could handle Mom being hurt. I grew up as her protector. I called the police on Dad. I threw coffee mugs at him when he was hurting her. I even tried bashing an iron skillet on his head once. Her tears had always unraveled me.

"Kathy," she whispered, as if ready to tell me a deep secret. "What will *you* do without me?"

It's about the two-year-old, echoed in my spirit. I wanted to tell Mom I had always done life without her. I wanted to tell her about Dad's abuse. I wanted to spill my soul. Little Kathy was bursting to share her pain. I wanted to tell her I had been terrified of her leaving me with Dad every night that she left for work. I was torn between the old pain and fear and the new work the Lord was doing in me.

I cupped her face with one hand and assured her, "*I'll* be okay, Mom. Really. *I'll* be okay." I couldn't have said that the day before, but remembering God's interaction with me on the road and on the massage table, I knew He'd take care of me. He knew why I was fearful, and somehow He would work things out.

The urgency with which she had held my eyes softened. Her grip relaxed. We cuddled for a long while then prayed and closed the chapter of that day.

The next morning began in a blur of startling events. Sitting by Mom's bed, having breakfast, I "saw" Dad. I mean, I saw him with the eyes of my heart—or maybe with the eyes of God's heart—as he peeked into the bedroom to see what we were doing.

"My gosh, Dad. You need a haircut!"

"I know. I called Adriena yesterday to see if she'd cut it."

Ouch! Here I was, a full-time caregiver, but Dad had to call a dear neighbor to cut his hair. My heart stung as if hit by a sharp dart. The change was taking shape in real time now.

Mom had always shaved the two-inch ring of hair that grew around Dad's otherwise bald head, but she hadn't been able to do it for months now. Curly hair, wildly out of control, was growing over and into his ears and way down his neck. His curly eyebrows had sprouted wings that actually stuck out over the bows of his glasses. Straight, stiff bristles sparsely covered the bald part of his head. Suddenly, for the first time in my life, I actually saw Dad as a broken, lost man, and my heart filled with compassion. *Compassion! For my dad!* God certainly was working in overdrive!

I saw his 140-pound frame, 45 pounds lost during Mom's three-year health decline. I saw the deep, worried wrinkles on his tired face. I saw the red bruised places under his thin, old skin, where he had bumped into things as he worked outside. I saw the thread-bare elbows of his flannel shirt and the hole in his left shoe. I saw a man losing his wife of sixty-three years. I saw his pronounced limp, arthritis crippling his right hip. A great pressure hit my chest again, but nothing like the pressure of that day on the highway. This was the pressure of a freshly lit love.

"I'm sorry you had to call Adriena, Dad. I'll cut your hair."

The grin that spread across Mom's face delighted me. The shock that hit Dad's face humbled me.

"I have no idea what I'm doing, but I'll get the stuff ready, and if you're brave enough, Dad, we'll do it."

We finished breakfast, and then he and I headed out onto the deck, into the warm summer sun. I plugged in the shaver, dug the small, sharp scissors out of the bottom of the bag, and turned toward Dad.

He slipped his T-shirt off and slid into the chair. A slight tremor moved through me, and I stepped backward, away from him. After several slow, deep breaths, I inched forward and turned on the shaver. I timidly placed my left hand on his head to tip it forward so that I could start on his neck. My heart jerked. My stomach lurched. Touching him ignited something in me like hot lightning. My left hand flew off Dad's head as if burned.

"Da-d, lea-an fo-r-ward a bit, p-pl-ease," I stuttered. My right hand trembled, thoughts ricocheted in my head. *I have to touch him. I have to smooth out the wrinkles so I don't cut him. Kathy! You can do this! Come on! Do this!*

I forced my left hand back to the base of his neck, stretching the skin a bit, carefully clearing one path with the razor. I tipped the razor to get rid of the hair but inadvertently dropped the tuft on Dad's shoulder. Automatically, I reached to brush it off like anyone would, but I froze. Absolutely froze! This was my Dad's bare shoulder.

I cleared one more path, and sure enough, that tuft landed next to the first, as if by cruel coincidence. I knew I had to do this. I cleared one more path, as if to get some momentum, and then with one finger, brushed off all three bunches. It sent an electric shudder through me that sucked the breath right out of me. I grabbed the deck rail to steady myself.

"It's about the two-year-old. Face this. I'm here with you. You can do this."

313

I recognized the Shepherd's voice and answered a silent and trembling *Okay*.

Every time my left hand touched Dad, I pictured my Savior's nail-scarred hand over mine, helping me, healing me, erasing my fear of Dad and the terror of his abusive sexual touch over so many years. When I thought my chest would burst, I imagined the Holy Spirit breathing in me and through me and with me—slow and steady.

It used to take Mom five minutes to cut Dad's hair and trim his eyebrows. By the time I finished that day, we were sunburned. I sank into bed that night totally spent and stretched beyond what I deemed possible. The Bible says that God never gives us more than we can handle, but I was pretty sure that He was badly overestimating my ability. I thanked Him that His mercies are new every morning, because I was sure going to need more mercy for the rest of this "two-year-old" stuff!

Sure enough, in His great grace, a surprise greeted me the next morning. As I watched Dad shuffle out of the bedroom, my heart warmed looking at his haircut and trimmed eyebrows. I hardly remembered the freaked-out part.

Baby steps, I thought and then smiled as I remembered that hilarious movie about baby steps called *What About Bob?* But this was no movie. This was my life. This was God slowly, carefully, giving me a heart for this violent, abusive man who was losing his wife.

Next, the Lord moved me to do something about Dad's thin frame. Mom, a great cook, would be impossible to replace, but I could begin while she was still alive to get recipes and learn the meals he liked best. Previously, that hadn't mattered one iota to me. This week, I actually desired to feed him well, to lift his spirits with some great meals that would put some meat back on his bones.

Ezekiel's words surfaced in my thoughts, how God removes the heart of stone and gives a heart of flesh. I had never been quite sure what that meant or how it would be accomplished, but right here, living with Mom and Dad, He was softening my heart one tiny step at a time, one small service at a time.

Most certainly, He was redeeming this threesome that had been intertwined in grievous, diabolical ways—Dad's mate when Mom worked nights and Mom's mate when he drank—twisted and sick, yes, but not beyond God's healing hands.

We all awaited the stroke that would take Mom and knew it lurked just around the corner; as the Lord was doing the last of the work in the two-year-old, I felt it would be soon. Thus, day by day, I began releasing Mom.

In the wee hours of the next morning I asked the Lord to give me a hint of when that fatal stroke would come. I had no idea at just how stunning His answer would be—just another confirmation of God's great grace and His constant presence with us.

Knowing He'd heard me, I pressed to cultivate this tiny love for Dad as quickly as I could, and I knew Mom was doing her own pressing as well. It had started a couple of months prior when I would peek into their bedroom to ask if she was ready for her coffee, and she'd answer, "Nope. Gotta read my promises. Gotta bad attitude," and she'd be holding a book full of God's promises that someone had assembled under topics like joy, hope, grief, or mercy.

I would simply nod and move into the kitchen and begin fixing breakfast. Every twenty minutes or so, I'd peek in to see if she was ready. The answer was always written on her face—a furrowed brow, with her nose still in her *Promise* book, or a childlike smile spreading from ear to ear and a finger inviting me to come closer. "You know," she'd whisper as if telling me a secret, "He's gone to prepare a place for me, and He's coming to take me there."

"Yep, Mom. That is so true." These were sweet, priceless moments for me and Mom, and boy did she enjoy her coffee once she got to that place of assurance again.

However, one morning I couldn't even ask the coffee question before she motioned me into the room, excited and breathless. "Kathy! Kathy! I've been fraternizing!"

"Yeah?" I answered, plopping on her bed to listen, my arm wrapped around her thin, bony shoulders.

"Oh, it's so beautiful there, and I had a long walk with Eddy and Douglas, I chatted with Aunt Ella and Uncle Ted, and I spoke with Mother and Father. And He's coming to take me there, to be with them and Him forever."

My heart thumped. I hugged her long and hard, knowing it may be the last hug. The stunning hint had come. Our final good-bye was at hand.

As I fixed her coffee, a sweet peace enveloped me. Eddy was my big brother who was killed by a drunk driver when he was twelve and I was ten. I knew how much I longed to see him, and I could only imagine how a mother would long to be reunited with her firstborn. Doug was Mom's first grandchild. His suicide in his twenties rocked our world like Eddy's death had. I could just see Mom walking and talking with them.

I had to smile that our precious Lord would orchestrate a meet 'n greet with those two first, then with the two who raised Mom the first ten years of her life.

Mom's brow never furrowed again. She lived on the fringes of heaven for the next six days. We all knew that stroke thirteen would hit at some point. We had lived for several years wondering each day when it would come. As God would have it, not long after my encounter with Him on the massage table, number thirteen hit, and it quickly became obvious that this would be the fatal stroke and the time for a radical obedience.

Sixty-three years of marriage and Mom's deep love for Dad caused her to doggedly repeat the same question that troubled her. With a thick, heavy tongue and through paralyzed lips, she asked for the last time, "Whl tkk cr u Rlf?"

Who will take care of Ralph? There it was again.

I gathered her limp, arthritic hands into mine and looked through her tired brown eyes, into her spirit where she was still strong.

"Mom, I will. I will take care of Dad. I will take care of him." The tenderness in my voice surprised me and Mom. Her crooked mouth twisted into a lopsided smile, and a slight twinkle replaced the fear that always accompanied each stroke.

I smiled too, and we held each other's eyes for precious minutes. Precious time—that silence that communicates a lifetime of things that can't be put into words. Healing. Hope. Forgiveness. Restoration. Faith in the faithful God whom we had shared for thirty years.

At last she heard what she so longed to hear. And, just in time, I could voice what she had prayed I *would* say. Lying beside her as her life on this earth slowly ended, I heard God speak Joel 2:25 (KJV) to me. "I will restore to you the years that the locust hath eaten."

The thirteenth stroke had hit but didn't bring a quick death. It moved into slow heart failure that lasted almost twelve hours, but we lived those tough hours in the strength of Mom's hope and God's great grace. We took turns lying on the bed with her. We sang praises. We told everyone who came to say good-bye about what God had given us.

And the most amazing thing was yet to come. The Lord was still not finished pouring out great love and mercy. About the sixth hour, my sister gently closed Mom's eyelids, not wanting to look into empty grey eyes any longer. A few hours later, Mom's breathing finally changed, and the instant the last tiny breath ended, her eyelids popped completely open, her normal light-brown eyes filled with sparkles, and she looked straight up above her.

Jesus, coming to take her home forever.

Breath was gone. Heavenly life had just begun.

Several years have passed since that glorious reunion of Mom and her Savior. Dad is ninety-one, and I continue to care for him because God's redeeming grace reached and healed the deepest fears of the two-year-old, bringing me into wholeness and peace.

And all is well.

"IT'S ABOUT THE TWO-YEAR OLD" –
FOR DEEPER THOUGHT . . .

1. Do you have a hurt from the past that surfaces sometimes? How can you begin to deal with it and receive healing?

2. For whom do you need to have "new" eyes? Perhaps it's someone you'd rather not be in relationship with, but with whom you *need* to be in relationship with for the good of your family or your colleagues or your success, etc. Brainstorm and write down some steps you can take to begin seeing that person differently.

3. How often do you take a little break to gather wisdom and strength for the tasks that you face? What changes do you think would take place if you set aside time like this regularly?

4. 2 Corinthians 9:8 says, "And God is able to make all grace abound to you, so that always having all sufficiency in everything, you may have an abundance for every good deed." How does this encourage you?

5. Romans 15:13 says, "Now may the God of hope fill you with all joy and peace in believing, so that you will abound in hope by the power of the Holy Spirit." What changes in yourself do you hope for? How can you begin to cooperate with the Lord as He makes those changes?

6. What do you do when you get weary and feel you can't go on? To whom or what do you turn? Jesus's invitation to take a break with Him is stated clearly in Matthew 11:28–30: "Come to Me, all who are weary and heavy-laden, and I will give you rest. Take My yoke upon you and learn from Me, for I am gentle and humble in heart, and YOU WILL FIND REST FOR YOUR SOULS. For My yoke is easy and My burden is light." How do these words from Jesus encourage you? What times during the day could you come aside and find rest in Him?

It's About the Two-Year-Old

To be broken bread, the wheat must be
crushed.
To be poured out wine, the grapes must be
pressed.
Oh God, here I am. I offer myself as a living
sacrifice.
Help me die to self so that others may live.
(Romans 12:1; John 12:24)

The Beginning of the End

I love bedtime. Closing the curtain on another day, having received the grace to get through it, is a sweet time. I take a quick glance toward tomorrow, knowing my Lord holds my life in His nail-scarred hands, feeling that peace that makes no sense. Another sunset that will be greeted by tomorrow's sunrise.

I flip the light off and bury myself under my thick down comforter, breathing in that scent of clean that comes from hanging outside and gathering the mountain breezes. I make a small tunnel for Barnabas, my silver-gray kitty, and cuddle him in close to me. As we snuggle, I visit with the Lord about the day and soon the rhythmic music of Barney's purr eases me into deep sleep. But without warning, a dream crashes in and throws me into a battle that will take two decades to win.

I am a silent spectator, watching the events unfurling before me. I see my parents, siblings, and myself, entering a spacious but unfamiliar room. Not an ordinary room—no signs that anyone lives there. No furniture. No lights. No decorations. Just a bare room of dark wooden walls covered with shelves and shelves of pictures. Pictures of us. Hundreds of them. Maybe thousands.

We shoot each other those "huh?" kind of looks that say, *"This can't be happening,"* and we spread out, inspecting this crazy collection of *our* moments.

Someone had documented our lives—had captured us at all ages, over three or four decades. I wander to the far end of the room and casually begin scanning pictures. After three or four dozen photos, I realize something is terribly wrong. I try to shake it off as mere coincidence, but I begin to tremble inside.

Sensing that I need time to absorb the secret that the photographs are whispering to me, I deliberately slow my pace. My trembling turns to fear. I hesitate to even look at the next column of shelves. Sucking in a long, deep breath, I pick up each picture, the next one heavier than the previous one. It's no coincidence. I am not in *any* picture.

Muffled, in the background, I hear my family chattering like school kids and laughing as they reminisce about the times that had been captured in these haunting prints. As I slowly work my way around the room, the fear turns to a dread that finally finds a voice.

"Hey, you guys. Where am I? I'm not in any of these pictures."

Silence.

Not a big deal, I think. *Maybe they didn't hear me.* I keep inching my way toward my family, running my finger over each picture, never finding myself. Desperation makes me shout this time.

"Hey, Mom! Where am I?"

No response.

They continue talking and laughing, telling stories and teasing one another. I break into their little circle and scream, "Where am *I*?"

No response. No recognition. Nothing.

I'm invisible! In the black silence of that revelation, I jerk my head toward a brilliant light streaming in from a floor-to-ceiling window that was not there when we entered the room. I float through it like vapor, into a golden field of dry stubble and dead weeds that stretches in every direction to the horizon.

"Where am I-I-I?" my cry echoes to the heavens. Eerie, heavy silence.

Now what? I wonder as I stand there waiting. Expecting something, actually.

Eventually, compelled forward, I notice something in the distance beginning to take shape. Mystified *and* afraid, I'm drawn toward it. I can't turn right or left. I can't turn around. I can't stop thinking about my family.

A small doll maybe?

I had never played with dolls. My dad and older brother, Eddy, were into sports, and they significantly shaped the course of my life. I could throw a ball before I could walk, and try as Mom did to buy dolls that I would like, they were just things to improve my throwing motion. Poor Mom.

Closer.

Yes, a doll, but bigger than it first appeared to be.

Then Mom tried dresses. Wadded up, they became pretty good projectiles as well, especially when Eddy was working with me. "You'll throw farther if you release a little higher," he'd explain. When I'd give him a blank look, he would demonstrate by mashing one of my three dresses into a wad and throwing it at the top of the door, any door, and that's where Mom usually found them hanging. Poor Mom.

A naked doll!

Finally, Mom gave up dresses and tried time with her in the kitchen. Well, for someone tickled with pleasing her big brother, you know how *that* went. Kitchens hold endless things to throw. Poor Mom.

A contorted doll. Arms and legs in odd positions.

Too close. Tiptoeing forward now. Fear rising.

Eddy and Dad loved to wrestle. Regardless of my size, I entered the fray just to be with Eddy. Poor, *poor* Mom.

I mean, I was the first girl in the Loudenburg genealogy in thirty-three years! The doc had warned Mom that she should expect all boys, and sure enough, she birthed Eddy first—*all* boy for sure. He could have been twins all by himself. I came next, Mom's second C-section. She swears that she shouted, "Yay, God!" the second she came to and heard she'd had a girl. They had chosen a boy's name and had to scramble to find a name for me.

As she watched the dolls and dresses fly in various directions and the three of us tumbling and rolling around on the living room floor like a big ball of tangled yarn, she may have wondered if number two *was* indeed a girl!

Not a doll at all!

Alive. Eyes bulging.

Can't breathe. Swallowed by terror.

Mouth frozen wide open as if screaming.

On my knees. Can't breathe. Pounding the ground. Can't breathe.

"Mom, where *were* you?" I squeak and waken.

Gulping in asthmatic wisps of air. Knees under me. Tucked in a tight ball. Pounding my pillow.

The soft clicking of the hallway clock helps me recover rhythmic breathing. Shallow, but rhythmic. Barnabas inches up close again, pressing his head into my sunken shoulders. Concentrating on his love and the soothing *tick-tock*, I roll onto my back and unknot myself. I run my hand over Barney's head and down his silver back, coaxing out that peaceful purr as I slowly return to some sense of sanity.

I am the little girl in that field.

"My Lord, what do I do with this?" I whisper into the night.

Tick-Tock, tick-tock, tick-tock.

Memories of my last months in Czechoslovakia drift into my mind. Zdenek, the father of one of my students, and I had worked hard in his vineyard to restore it. We ripped out all the dead roots and cut off all the dead clusters and branches. As Zdenek axed out the deepest rotten root, the Lord moved powerfully in my spirit. Through Deuteronomy, He spoke to me of a root that bears poisonous fruit. So right then and there, I had asked Him to rip that root from within me.

"Thank You, Lord, for making that connection. This dream has everything to do with that root, doesn't it? Please sever it and help me cooperate in the process. Amen."

Bedtime. Closing the curtain on another day, trusting God's grace to get me through to the next sunrise. The dream assaults me again, tearing me out of deep sleep, but the accompanying fear is slightly diminished by the sense that it has great purpose, if I will just walk through it, one day at a time.

I wake and shake it out of my mind as much as possible so that I can prepare for the day. I have the best job in the world, teaching middle school Language Arts. Each day is an adventure, filled with endless possibilities. Truly, the thrill of teaching keeps me pressing forward on the days when I can barely breathe.

Another day wonderfully spent, but I'm a little apprehensive to go to bed. The terror of that dream is still fresh, and I only have a clue of what it really means.

I cuddle in with Barnabas, ask the Lord about that root, and drift off to sleep.

A second dream crashes in. A small spider, covered with coarse hair, crawls out of the corner of the room and moves toward me. As it presses me against the walls, I scream and awake.

I slide back under the covers, but I don't go back to sleep. "Lord, these are related aren't they?" I ask. "I don't know how they're connected to the root thing, but You do. Please tell me what to do next."

After a week of these two terrifying dreams, my friend gives me the name of a Christian counselor. I call her immediately and relay an abridged version of my nightmares. She then calls another friend, and the three of us begin meeting once a week.

I begin by telling Anne and Ruth about my brother's death and how the Lord had healed that pain, about how He had dealt with my lesbian tendencies, and about my missionary time in Czech for three years. I tell them especially about my time with Zdenek in his vineyard; I tell them how he axed out old, dead roots, and the Spirit reminding me of Deuteronomy 29:18. I tell them that I asked the Lord right then and there to get the poisonous root out of my life, and that these dreams are probably related to that prayer.

"Tell us more about the dreams, Kathy," Anne encourages.

With some effort, I unfold them in detail.

"Well, let's pray and ask the Lord what He has in mind," Anne invites.

We drop our heads and quiet our hearts. Anne's prayer is simple. "Lord, what would you like to do here?" We listen.

Reconnect is what I hear but am not sure what to do with it, so I wait.

Ruth finally looks up. "Kathy, you must reconnect with 'little Kathy'. Does that mean anything to you?"

"Yeah. I think I heard the word *reconnect* too, though I have no idea of how to do it."

So we bow our heads and pray. After some time, Anne takes my hand and looks deeply into my expectant eyes. "Let's begin walking toward little Kathy." Ruth nods in agreement.

"Let's go back to that house with the Lord," Anne begins.

The dreams have been so vivid and persistent, that I have no trouble imagining that I'm in that field, the strange house with all the pictures behind me and the terrified doll-like Kathy in the distance.

I look at her, and instantly every muscle tenses. My chest constricts, making it hard to breathe, like a severe asthma attack.

"It's okay, Kathy. The Lord's with us," Anne breaks in. "You're not alone. Can you take a step toward little Kathy?"

I inch forward, but the terror in her silent scream and wide eyes seizes me. Somehow, it's mine. I gasp and wheeze and fall into Anne's lap unconscious.

Eventually aware of soft mumbling, I slowly realize Anne and Ruth are praying for me. I'm soothed by their voices. When

I finally open my eyes, Anne pats my cheek and says, "It's okay, Kathy. The Lord's here with us. He knows what He's doing."

"I'm n-not sure I w-want to do this," I stammer and sit up. "Why couldn't I breathe, Anne?"

"Well, sometimes, when something horrible happens, people can disassociate with themselves. It's kind of like going somewhere else until what's happening to them stops."

Silence. My mind trying to process her words.

"Something painful happened when you were really young, and as you took that step, you experienced a bit of little Kathy's pain."

"I don't know if I can take another step today. Can we try again next week?" I ask.

"You bet. Let's pray before you go."

Over the next several months, I take about a dozen steps toward that frozen, miniature figure. Even though it feels like progress, the dreams still haunt me night after night. I always scream in terror. I always have the same story for Anne and Ruth, and I'm tired. Just plumb worn out.

And then the dreams stop. Just like that.

I'm relieved for the break, though I know the Lord's not done.

During these lengthy interludes, I begin asking Mom questions, her answers always shocking me and telling me things that I *need* but don't want to know.

"I've never had asthma have I?"

"Yeah, you did. It began when you were two."

"Susan Mathews was our only babysitter, right?"

"No, Jess and Sarah's two college sons babysat a lot."

I realize the Lord is putting things together piece by piece, like a giant jigsaw puzzle.

And then the dreams begin again.

Anne and her husband, Paul, are God's provision for this next season of healing, and we begin where we always begin, in the field, inching toward little Kathy. I have some trepidation, but I know I will always "come to" after I pass out. I know the dreams are instruments God's using for my good. I know God is making progress on the poisonous root that has crippled me for decades without me knowing it even existed.

With each step, I cautiously assimilate little Kathy's terror. Reconnecting with someone and something I do not know, but must discover. Although this reconnection is always brutal, at least the dreams begin loosening their grip. And I get closer and closer to little Kathy with each exhausting session.

The dreams stop once again, and life resumes with no thoughts of little Kathy.

When they return for the third time, we begin again.

"Kathy, you are so close now. With just a few more steps, I think you can make contact today," Paul encourages.

I suck all the air out of the room and whisper, "Okay."

A few more steps. I bend over and extend my hand to little Kathy, absolutely unable to lift her into my arms due to the labored breathing crushing my chest. In a heartbeat, however, she grabs one of my fingers like little kids do, her screaming mouth softens into a smile, and her wide eyes once full of terror, glisten with joy.

"Yikes!" I shout and jump off the couch, scaring Paul and Anne half to death. "She's alive! She's alive!" Chattering a million words a minute, I tell them what just happened. "*I'm* alive! Anne! I am alive! No passing out this time! We're connected!"

Sure, it's only one little hand grasping one finger, but we'd been at this for over a decade, so it is precious. Priceless.

That very night the spider dream changes. I'm watching it come at me, but it's only as big as a dinner plate, and someone behind me kills it with a piece of heavy pipe. I turn to see who it is, and all I can see is that marvelous light—the same light that first created the door in the strange house with all the pictures of our family.

Over the next several years, God put faces and names to all the sexual abuse those dreams represented, but without the terror.

My sweet Savior, Jesus, had heard my prayer in Zdenek's vineyard, and He had unearthed and cut out the poisonous root that had borne so much bad fruit over the course of my life. He did it slowly, gently, only as much as I could handle— season by season—and a few months after I said good-bye to Anne and Paul, He brought it to conclusion.

During worship at a retreat, the Spirit enabled me to stoop down, wrap little Kathy in my arms, and lift her up. As I hugged her, she melted into me. Oh, the sweetness of that moment. As I twirled round and round in rejoicing and wholeness, words from Isaiah resounded in my soul. *Jesus came to proclaim liberty to captives and to set the prisoners free.*

And the Spirit whispered, "It is finished."

"THE BEGINNING OF THE END" – FOR DEEPER THOUGHT . . .

Dreams often mean nothing, and we usually don't remember most of them. However, God often spoke to people in the Bible through dreams. In Genesis, Joseph had a dream as a boy, and it came to pass—step by step—until he was second in command to Pharaoh. Daniel had dreams and could interpret them. The book of Daniel chronicles them clearly. In the New Testament, the Lord told Joseph in a dream to take Mary and baby Jesus to Egypt to escape King Herod's plot to kill him.

If a dream is from the Lord, it will not go against Scripture, and it will lead toward good. It will bring healing, positive actions, godly character, and a closer walk with Jesus.

1. If you have ever had a recurring dream, how did you deal with it? What were the results?

In Daniel 2:17, we see how David dealt with a dream that the king had. He asked his friends to ask for mercy from God in heaven concerning the meaning of the dream. In the night, God gave Daniel the meaning, and Daniel praised God for His wisdom and power. Daniel believed in God and trusted Him for the interpretation. If you are a believer, you, too, can ask God to reveal the meaning of a dream.

2. What trusted friends can you ask to pray with you if you have a dream? How can you prepare yourself to seek God's wisdom and mercy?

3. Later in Daniel 10, the answer to Daniel's prayers about the meaning of a dream is delayed quite a long time. How well prepared are you to wait on the Lord and trust His timing? When have you waited on the Lord in the past? What were the results?

4. How willing are you to pray for a godly counselor to help you do the work that the dream may suggest? If you don't have someone you can trust, how willing are you to begin praying for God to send you the right person to help you?

5. Psalm 34:18 says, "The Lord is near to the brokenhearted and saves those who are crushed in spirit." Have you given your life to the Lord so that He can come near and walk you through the process of healing? If not, take some time to read and reread this Scripture and record what has kept you from surrendering to Him.

The Beginning
of The End

You know my name and the hairs on my head.
You know my thoughts before I speak them.
You know my pain, and the scars of my heart
And You gather my tears.
(Matthew 10:30; Psalm 94:11, 56:8)

Conclusion

"Whose Eyes"
(written in 1988)

The blood-soaked pajamas screamed
for attention.
The battered bicycle yelled at me
for care.
The scarlet-stained pavement yanked me
like a merciless magnet.
The empty bedroom whispered threats
of loneliness and despair.

At ten, the casket held my life, now death,
and I too was buried there.

No words spoken
as if they were not there,
Submersion in silent grief
that somehow was sinful to share.
Silent entities –
crippled and alone –
We traveled the next tortuous miles
as if our hearts were suddenly stone.
Anger and hate

became close friends.
Pretending gave birth to separateness,
and security unraveled at the ends.
Hiding behind activity
became the thing to do
As if it would, like magic,
cause the pain to be subdued.
At seventeen, honor student and all, yet
a tiny creature really wondering,
"Who indeed are you without your big brother?"

Time passes
and spoken words are still few.
Yet each new day speaks within
of something made anew.
The Christ of the cross
reaches deep –
He touches the wound
and helps it to seep
With all that is hidden there
Though the family still can't share.

Pain that has been healed
brings a mysterious depth,
And while the scar remains,
no secrets need be kept.
Why do we avoid the sharing
when we all know the same pain?
Maybe words are still too awkward
and yet, just the same,

How I long for the next tenuous step
When, as a family, healing and words will have met.

My eyes at ten
were too newly formed to see
That tragic loss
is something that can be
so great a step toward maturity.

My eyes as a teen
were blinded by loneliness and pain.
They could not see
what there was to gain
by enduring a loss that seemed only to maim.

Now my eyes, many years later,
sparkle with the knowledge of God
Who gently reaches in and heals
the rips and tears where pain has trod.

Note from the Author

Just before this book went to press, the Lord moved again in a beautiful way. It happened on a cool June evening in 2016.

As I was serving Dad his dinner, his head suddenly fell into his hands. At ninety-one years old, he was a broken, contrite man. His tears soaked his pants, and he mumbled over and over, "You don't deserve this. I'm so sorry." His heart finally softened. Mine completely healed. Leaning forward, kneeling before Dad, I wrapped my arms around him, cheek to cheek. Holding him, rocking him, I kept saying, "You're forgiven, Dad."

It has taken eleven years of caregiving to bring Dad and me to this complete restoration. God finally broke Dad's heart and in that moment set my heart completely free. My love for Dad had died in my childhood, but in these priceless moments . . . on my knees . . . rocking him . . . God flooded my heart with a profound love for Dad. Words I never thought I could or would ever say.

"No eye has seen, no ear has heard, no mind has conceived what God has prepared for those who love him" (1 Corinthians 2:9). Thank you, sweet Jesus!

About the Author

Kathy is a passionate teacher and a powerful speaker. Her career as an educator spans thirty years and every age group. From an abusive childhood, her brother's fatal accident, her lesbianism, and suicide attempt, she has learned the power of God's healing love and redemptive grace. Kathy's missionary experience has reinforced the truth that the Holy Spirit's gifts are freely given to those who are surrendered and available. Living with her parents as their full-time caregiver has strengthened her conviction that the teeth of grace can restore anything that the locusts have eaten (Joel 2:25). Helping others put feet to their faith and finding strength for the days ahead is the heart of her message.

Ordering Information

You can order copies of this book at:

Kathy@LivingontheThinnestEdge.com
www.livingonthethinnestedge.com
[under construction]